# the frugal MILLIONAIRES

# the frugal MILLIONAIRES

70 millionaires anonymously
share their ideas about money
to help each other and you.

## JEFF LEHMAN

**MENTOR**
PRESS LLC

Seattle, Washington

ISBN: 978-0-9768999-2-1
Library of Congress Control Number: 2008906236

First Edition, First Printing
Printed on recycled paper in the United States of America

Quantities of this book are available at a volume discount.
For more information, please contact:
publisher@MentorPressLLC.com

Editing: Christine Willmsen
Cover Design: Ryan Michael Scott
Interior Design: Soundview Design Studio

**MENTOR**
**PRESS LLC**

Seattle, Washington
www.MentorPressLLC.com
www.TheFrugalMillionaires.com

# Thank You

---

To DMG, SLL, DRG for your inspiration, and JBM for your curiosity.

To all the frugal millionaires who contributed their ideas anonymously:

A&JB, AA, AC, AD, B&GH, BEH, C&LM, DAS, DC, DES, DLM, DLS, DMG, DRG, DTA, ERK, FJC, GG, J&CB, J&MD, JC, JDS, JED, JKB, JLL, JMM&DRS, JSB, JT&B, JTA, KJH, L&AO, MCE, MG&DG, MHS&AW, MJM, MSG, MW, NM&JPR, PMM, R&DW, RDF, RJC, RME, RP, RSM, S&AW, SLL, SR&BS, TFM, T&RR, V&NH, VNN, VRN, VTN, WAL and WCA.

To Mom and Dad, for passing along the frugal genes to Jon and me.

And, to all of you readers who are looking for practical, common sense ways to grow your wealth.

---

# Creating *The Frugal Millionaires*

It's funny how things happen sometimes. This book project started with me asking a former girlfriend, who was a recently retired software millionaire, for a list of things she did to make her money work smarter for her. We agreed that if she gave me her list, I'd give her mine. There were many great ideas on her list that had never occurred to me. I used one of her ideas to immediately make a change to my retirement portfolio and saw an instant benefit. Thank you!

Next, I asked a friend of mine, a retired accountant millionaire, for his list. Being an accountant his list was meticulous. We had the same deal, we'd trade lists. There were more ideas I had never considered.

I then asked a trusted millionaire friend of many years, who had transitioned from real estate into technology, to do the same. He offered all kinds of new ideas and perspectives as well. This little idea sharing exercise was beginning to get interesting…and it was saving me money.

I mentioned that I was doing this list sharing exercise to a young "millionaire-in-training" friend. He immediately asked, "May I have a look at those lists?" "No, not yet," I said, "they're all going to be part of a book…someday!"

I then asked myself one question:

> If I could expand my group of three frugal millionaire friends and get even more ideas on how to think about money, would this be a practical and common sense way to help shorten everyone's path to growing their wealth?

Everyone I asked thought networking with millionaires and sharing their frugal ideas was a great concept...plus they wanted a copy of the book! And so the idea for *The Frugal Millionaires* was born.

*Why would busy millionaires want to participate in this project?*

To do the research for *The Frugal Millionaires* I networked to uncover as many frugal millionaires as I could. Ultimately, 70 of them contributed anonymously to this book. They were generous with their time and ideas. I am immensely grateful to them.

The motivation for these frugal millionaires was simple: They would put their ideas in and get even more ideas back from other like-minded millionaires. Then, I'd write a book so the frugal millionaires could help others know what they know, and in the end, everyone would get smarter about their money.

Not surprisingly, this powerful network of frugal millionaires gave me over 800 practical and useful ideas, but not a single one of them came up with every idea that I'm reporting here. That's one of the big reasons they participated in the research...so they could find out what they didn't know and learn from others. Very smart.

Money is just about basic math and common sense to the frugal millionaires. The concept of growing wealth is pretty simple to understand in its basic form, but executing on it can really mess people up. So why not let those who have been there already show the way? They know that money needs to be given proper respect. Plus, they have no reason not to share what they know with those who are willing to listen and who are open to making some changes in how they think about their money. Sharing ideas like this doesn't create any competitive disadvantage to the people giving the information...in fact, it helps everyone.

*The motivation*

I've written this book to simply "give back" and share ideas with people who want to do better with their money. It might sound trite, but it's true. And, I have no political, religious, business or hidden agendas that I'm trying to push on you with this book. I didn't find this to be true in some of the other personal finance books I have read!

OK, maybe there is one agenda that I do want to get across:

*Everyone (even millionaires) can be smarter with their money. Don't waste it! Period.*

I'm not trying to sell you anything other than your small investment in this book and that should be more than recovered in a very short time by just applying a few of the concepts, ideas and best practices you'll read. Yes, it's all really that simple. And why shouldn't it be?

The social and monetary costs of investing in this book have been kept to a minimum by only printing low-cost paperback editions on recycled paper. After expenses, a portion of the profits of this book will be donated anonymously to groups selected by the contributors. As you'll read in the pages ahead, giving back is something that is very important to all these frugal millionaires. When they give, they get back even more. They wouldn't have it any other way.

Enjoy growing your wealth.

Jeff Lehman
Seattle, Washington

---

# Table of Contents

# Disclaimer

---

I am not an accounting, financial or legal advisor. The information in this book is simply a window into how a select group of millionaires have grown their wealth. You'd be silly not to listen to them, but it is your choice. Before making any financial decisions always talk to someone who is neutral and knowledgeable about money, and whose professional opinion you trust. Make sure they don't have a vested interest in profiting from any of the decisions you make. It's your money, your decisions, and your financial future, so choose wisely.

---

# Preface

Frugality is making a comeback, but some people will tell you that it never left town. Those are the people you are about to hear from. Frugality is both timeless and timely, and everyone can use it to their advantage.

There are millions of people who can't seem to get a grip on their money and feel that success is defined by what they own, without considering what they owe. This book will help keep you from being one of them. It will also help you if you already are one.

America is maxed out financially. This is not new news. We buy stuff we don't need. We willingly fall for the powerful marketing gimmicks out there that tell us we aren't cool, great parents, good looking, or smart unless we buy whatever marketers happen to be pitching. Or, that there is some quick path to endless wealth. There isn't.

We are the world's largest debtor nation. That's not good. We often buy things that make no sense for us to buy based on our current finances. At the end of the day, we are responsible for our own spending habits. No excuses. And now many people are paying the price for being irresponsible. Some may be able to fool the Joneses for a while, but all they are really doing is fooling themselves. This book is about how not to be one of them.

There is an oasis that many have found to protect themselves from getting into financial messes. It's called frugality. Frugality gets a bad rap from those who think they
are above practicing it. Some think being frugal means
being cheap. It doesn't, as you will see in the pages ahead,
but that's the sound bite that most people who can't control themselves financially have come up with to write off
frugality as a possible answer to their problems.

*Being frugal is smarter than being cheap.*

There are a core group of people who have gone against
the grain by not accepting over-spending as the great
American pass-time. They are the kind of people you
would least expect to be concerned about money. They are
millionaires. *Correction:* They are *frugal* millionaires.
They are healthy, wealthy and wise. They are painlessly
growing their net worth with their frugal ways. They are
about to tell you how they think differently about money
compared to most other people. You can freely use their
ideas to help keep more of what you earn, and grow it.

*In Lehman's Terms* is a series of author rants and raves on various money related topics. They are located throughout the book.

## *In Lehman's Terms:*
## I LOST IT ALL... SO NOW I'M A FINANCIAL EXPERT?

This is not to be confused with "rags to riches" stories which are always great to hear, but there are also plenty of stories about the "I made it all, I lost it all, and I made it all again" types of "millionaires." We all seem to thrive on a good "I was an underdog" story.

Those who have "lost it all and made it all again" seem to have cemented themselves into the urban myth of being credible financial experts because they've been to the dark side financially. This makes for great reading in personal finance books and magazines, but this wouldn't necessarily impress the frugal millionaires who have continued to grow their net worth and have *never* lost it all.

Aren't the millionaires who have kept and grown their net worth the ones you *really* want to learn from? If you had it all and lost it all you probably never had a very good hold on it to begin with, or you would have protected it and grown it, right? Right! Think of it this way: Would you want a doctor doing brain surgery on you who's last patient got an "accidental" lobotomy and later died?

# CHAPTER I

# The 2% Club

Depending on who's research you use or believe, the number of millionaires in the United States is anywhere from 1% to 3% of the population. We'll just split the difference and call them *The 2% Club*.

Research is fascinating because it can be viewed in so many ways. It can be extremely helpful, painfully boring or twisted and one-sided. I'll be providing you some basic statistical information on the frugal millionaires so you can get a feel for them (and how they might be more like you than you think), but it's the practical and common sense based ideas they provide that will ultimately give you the most value.

What do the frugal millionaires who contributed to this book know about money that the rest of us don't? As it turns out, they know plenty...yet they aren't obsessed or greedy about money at all. Once you've read this book you might have a completely different picture in your mind of what a millionaire looks like (a frugal one at least!). The difference is that these frugal millionaires take what they know about growing wealth and put it into action every day while the rest of us just continue doing what we are doing and wonder why we aren't getting ahead.

None of the 70 frugal millionaires who contributed are over-the-top flashy or have big egos. They are "everyday" millionaires. Some do have very nice homes and cars (and probably spent far less on them than what you might think they did), but that's all relative to their net worth. They are all definitely "members in good standing" of *The 2% Club*.

You could be sitting right next to one of the frugal millionaires and not even know they had any money. They don't fit the over-hyped media stereotype of millionaires and that's the way these frugal millionaires like it. They've got better things to do than constantly count their money, but they are very aware of how useful it is and how to make it work smart for them. They fly below the notoriety radar while basking in the glow of long-term financial security and freedom. They are rich *and* comfortable, and you are about to find out how they do it.

*In Lehman's Terms:*
## LOTTERY MILLIONAIRES

There are those "millionaires" who become brief members of *The 2% Club*....they are the lottery winners. You see it happen all the time. They win big, and for some of them, the first thing they do is go out and buy 20 cars they've always "needed" or houses for almost everyone in the family.

Very few, if any of them, hire a financial advisor to help them secure their future. Maybe the lottery executives should require that these "winners" get financial counseling before getting a dime of the money? Nope, then they would spend it on boring stuff and that wouldn't be marketable to the hopes and dreams of a typical lottery customer, so why bother, right?

Those winners that do hire honest advisors to help them have done the right thing. And some have done just that. But others become broke again in short order. Why? They just revert back to what they know about money. Absolutely nothing, other than how to waste it!

*Note to self*: Even though I don't play the lottery, when a large sum of money comes randomly my way (inherited or otherwise) it might make sense for me to devise a plan on how to: 1) enjoy it wisely, and 2) make it last a long time. The two are not mutually exclusive.

---

CHAPTER II

# How the frugal millionaires think differently about money than the rest of us

*"If life has taught me anything, it's that ninety-five percent of the people are always wrong."*

– dying billionaire Edward Cole (as played by Jack Nicholson), from the movie The Bucket List (2007)

To get rich you don't necessarily have to be brilliant, but to stay rich you need to have a brilliant plan...and you need to stick to it. The frugal millionaires think differently about money than the rest of us. They weren't necessarily born with their wealth growing traits. Some picked up these concepts from their parents, grandparents and other family members, some learned by observing others, or they just figured it out on their own.

For the frugal millionaires it comes down to just six simple concepts:

1) **Delayed gratification is easy for them**.

They can effectively block the "impulsive" gene in their bodies so that they don't ever "need something right now" (unless it is emergency medical care). They don't over-spend or over-leverage themselves, ever. They can wait to acquire stuff, if they acquire it at all.

**2) Resourcefulness in getting what they want is a key to their success.**

Once they do decide they need something they figure out the smartest and least costly way of getting it. They think and plan before they act. This might take a little of their time, but it is well worth it. They realize their time is more valuable than money but they don't put excessive convenience ahead of value received.

**3) They make living way below their means painless.**

They could buy a lot more of everything, but instead they choose not to play that game. They don't feel that they are making any sacrifices to do so. In fact, they take deep pride in not wanting what everyone else thinks they absolutely need.

**4) They don't like wasting anything (especially money).**

Just because they have money doesn't mean that they have to be excessive about using it. This is core to their thinking. If they don't waste their money then they also won't waste things like water, fuel, time, food and other resources. It's all interconnected for them.

**5) Their sense of "self-entitlement" is highly minimized.**

They don't use every opportunity to say "But I want it! I deserve it!" They will reward themselves when the time is right, and those rewards can be big, but they won't do it at the expense of their long term financial goals. They can keep the basic human drive of wanting to acquire more stuff just to show superiority over others at bay.

6) **Spending is OK with them, depending on what they are buying.**

They don't mind spending money as long as that means *investing* it in something. And, it's not always about financial investments. It could mean investing in people or things, with the goal of creating a certain outcome that makes the world a better place. It's not that they spend, but rather how they spend.

The frugal millionaires take these six simple concepts and do more than just think about how helpful they might be...*some day*...they do them *right now, every day.*

With all due respect to the band B.T. Express, who had the hit song "Do It ('Til You're Satisfied)" in 1975, I now offer you:

## The Frugal Millionaires Theme Song
Sung poorly to the melody of "Do It ('Til You're Satisfied)"

Go on be frugal
Be frugal, be frugal 'til you're satisfied
Whatever it is
Save it, save it 'til you're satisfied
Go on invest it
Invest it, invest it 'til you're satisfied
Whatever it is
Be frugal and show your resourceful side

Frugals know just what they'd like to do
Whatever it is don't waste it as long as it pleases you
Make it last as long as you can
When your through it's up to you to invest some more again

Go on and grow it
Grow it, grow it 'til you're satisfied
Whatever it is
Give it, give it 'til you're satisfied
Go on be frugal
Be frugal, be frugal 'til you're satisfied
Whatever it is
Be frugal and show your responsible side

Uh-Huh!

*In Lehman's Terms:*
## THE MEDIA AND MILLIONAIRES

There is a picture that the media paints of the so-called wealthy and famous. It's a picture of flashy people, who make and spend a lot of cash...and have the "I can always make more, so what do I care?" attitude. Many people want to be like this because this behavior appears to be glorified and rewarded in the media.

These generally short term wealthy types would rather spend their money getting noticed than staying wealthy.

Consider this cocktail party chatter:

Faux Wealthy Person says: *Check out my new pair of $1,325 carbon fiber sunglasses! They are so cool! I just charged them at Barney's. Have you been traveling lately? I just got back from a last minute (= expensive) trip to Monte Carlo. Oh, and I just leased a new Mercedes. My life is going well! Hey, how about you? How are you doing?*

Frugal Wealthy Person responds: *How fun for you. I'm doing well. My life is far less exciting than yours when it comes to abusing my credit card! But I did just pay off my mortgage. And, I'm flying to France for a month, on frequent flyer miles, to go hang with the locals. When I return I'm going to pay cash for a nice, gently used, fuel efficient, three-year-old foreign car. I'm debt free. Are you really sure that you are doing well?*

Which person would you rather be? Waste and excess are never a sound financial strategy.

---

# CHAPTER III

# Being frugal is smarter than being cheap

---

*Definitions of* **Frugal***: 1) Economical in use or expenditure; prudently saving or sparing; not wasteful. 2) Entailing little expense; requiring few resources. Synonyms: thrifty, careful.*

*Definitions of* **Cheap***: 1) Embarrassingly stingy. 2) Worthy of no respect. 3) Tastelessly showy. Synonyms: ungenerous, chintzy, flashy.*

*(SOURCE: Dictionary.com, with edits)*

Obviously, there's a big difference between the two, but most people don't make the distinction.

One of the frugal millionaires offered this illustration:

*Instead of going to lunch at a super high-end restaurant to celebrate a milestone the frugal millionaire might pick a mid-level one that has great food and fantastic service. They might even tip a few extra bucks because they know that extra $2 means more to their waitperson than it does to them right now. A cheap person wouldn't leave a tip, no matter where they ate lunch. And a really cheap per-*

*son wouldn't bring their wallet to lunch and then proba-
bly stick you for the meal.*

From Wikipedia:

> *Frugality* is the practice of acquiring goods and serv-
> ices in a restrained manner, and resourcefully using
> already owned economic goods and services, to
> achieve a longer term goal.
>
> *Frugality* in the context of certain belief systems, is a
> philosophy in which one does not trust, or is deeply
> wary of "expert" knowledge, often from commercial
> markets or corporate cultures, claiming to know what
> is in the best economic, material, or spiritual interests
> of the individual.

Bottom Line: *Frugal is smart. Cheap is dumb.*

———————

# CHAPTER IV

# Who are the frugal millionaires?

Finding the frugal millionaires was an exercise in resourcefulness. They don't have a blinking neon green "dollarsign" light on their foreheads. Some of the 140 potential people targeted to participate in this book weren't ultimately millionaires yet – but they were working on it. Some had the "millionaire aura" with nice house(s) and cars, great jobs, charming personalities and well-honed hobbies and vacationing skills. But they turned out to not be millionaires at all...and some might never be based on their financial priorities. Others were modest millionaires who didn't want to expose themselves financially despite all the confidentiality assurances. And, some chose to simply not respond. The net result was a 50% response rate...which is fantastic for any research project.

As mentioned, the frugal millionaires contributed anonymously. They didn't know who the other contributors were. The common denominator between all of them was their frugality and their willingness to share information with each other and you.

One frugal millionaire who participated sat next to me on a flight (*no, not in first class*) and noticed that I was working on the questionnaire for this book. When we were shutting down our laptops prior to landing he mentioned that he normally didn't look at other people's computer screens, but that he and his wife would be happy to participate. It's great that they did. They are true frugal geniuses.

There were two key qualifiers to be included in this book:

**1) The millionaires had to have a minimum net worth of a $1 million,** *not including their primary residence.* Why? While your house is an investment of sorts, it is still your home. You have to live somewhere. If the real estate that you own is earning recurring revenue, well, that's a true investment.

It's the net worth outside of their primary residence that gives this group of millionaires more flexibility to invest their money in an economic downturn and increase their wealth over the long run. All participants confirmed the minimum net worth requirements in writing.

**2) These millionaires had to be "frugal."** They answered numerous questions to confirm this. On any given day however, their definition of frugal might be somewhat different than yours. Hand-in-hand with the frugality qualifier was a very vivid display of common sense when it came to their relationship with money. That came out in the ideas that you will read further along in the book. Many of us think we are frugal and have common sense when it comes to money, but this group defines what it really means to do both well.

On a scale of 1 (least frugal) to 10 (most frugal), the group averaged a 6.78 score in the self assessment of their frugality. This shows that they have a very good sense of awareness when it comes to their money habits.

There were also other variables that helped in determining how frugal they are:

When it came to being frugal:

- 100% of them are self defined as being frugal.
- 90% said that it is important to be frugal no matter how much money you have.
- 75% said that frugality was inherited from their parents.
- 74% said they are frugal because it buys them more time or freedom.
- 73% said they are frugal because they don't like to waste anything.
- 73% said they are proud of being frugal.
- 69% said they like to hang around with other frugal people.
- 54% said they learned their sense of frugality on their own.
- 52% said they were frugal because regardless of how much money they had they didn't want people to think they could take advantage of them.
- 51% said they learned their sense of frugality from watching others.

Their family financial backgrounds were the following:

- 84% come from middle class families.
- 12% come from wealthy families.
- 4% come from poor families.

Interestingly, even those in the "wealthy" family group weren't millionaires because they had inherited it at a young age. Like the rest of the frugal millionaires they didn't become wealthy themselves until much later in life.

The ages of all the contributors ranged from 21 to 53 when they first became millionaires. Their age range when the research was conducted was 31 to 60 years old, with an average age of 48. The average time they have been a millionaire is 9 years.

*Other findings:*

- 83% of the millionaires are married.
- 75% are male
- 25% are female.

When it came to "giving back" here is what they said:

- 100% said they donate money to charities or causes.
- 54% said they like going to charity events.

This group was not just "flash-in-the-pan" millionaires. During the time that they have been millionaires the majority of them have seen their net worth grow.

- 91.4% have seen their net worth increase.
- 7.1% have seen their net worth stay about the same.
- 1.4% have seen their net worth decrease (that's just one person).

They live in California, Florida, Georgia, Illinois, Massachusetts, Montana, New York, North Carolina, Tennessee, Texas, Washington, and the United Kingdom.

The jobs these millionaires have are all varied, but are not necessarily considered the typical millionaire "jobs" like: trust fund babies, inheritors of daddy's real estate holdings, Fortune 500 CEOs, rock stars, movie stars, and professional athletes, etc.

They hold jobs in these fields: accounting, medicine, dentistry, aerospace consulting, media sales, high-tech, marketing, ophthalmology, law, public service, higher education, software, micro-finance, financial services, consulting, information technology, staffing & outsourcing, internet media, real estate, online dating services, uniform supply, management services, technology, management consulting, metal reselling, plumbing repair and contracting services, entrepreneurship, online search, commercial real estate, tradeshows and conferences, investments, authoring, sales consulting, software engineering, real estate development, software sales, online commerce, behavioral marketing and pharmaceuticals. Some had previously owned their own company.

Most worked full time or part time. There were a few who were fortunate enough to have retired early, but by no means were they idling away their time doing nothing.

If your perception of millionaires is that they are ruthless, money grubbing pigs...please give this group an opportunity to change your mind. These frugal millionaires are not obsessively focused on money. They are not greedy. These are the invisible millionaires that you might never notice. There are plenty of them out there. In this group very few of them placed "finances" at the top of a list of important priorities they were asked to rank. On the surface, that might make sense since they already have established their wealth. But chances are they have always been this way and gracious about their successes. They were asked to rank the following five attributes in order of importance using a scale of 1 (most important) to 5 (least important) and only using each of the numbers 1, 2, 3, 4, or 5 once.

Here is what they said:

1. Family – 1.19 average
2. Friends – 2.71 average
3. Freedom – 2.96 average
4. Finances – 3.82 average
5. Fun – 4.16 average

*Commentary*: A quick word about "fun" ranking last on the list. Don't think that this is an un-fun, stodgy group. All five of the above attributes were considered important. Given that family, friends and freedom are more important than finances means that there has to be a lot of fun happening in their lives, it just wasn't as important as the other attributes.

Other interesting statistics:

- 100% are not regular smokers. (Just three smoked an occasional cigar or cigarette.)

  *NOTE: This was a fascinating statistic. Draw your own conclusions, but common sense, desire for good health and a long life, and the recurring cost of expensive cigarettes are just three reasons that come to mind to support this result.*

- 60% believed that having a pre-nuptial agreement was a good idea.
- 57% used a financial advisor.
- 50% had a revocable / living trust in place.
- 10% had attended a "free" money making seminar with topics like: how to make money in real estate, or how to think like a millionaire, etc.

*In Lehman's Terms:*
## WHY THE PAPARAZZI WON'T STALK FRUGAL MILLIONAIRES

Have you noticed that the paparazzi don't stalk frugal millionaires when they go to the bank to deposit profits from successful investments? And they aren't there at the brokerage firm, or bank, video taping the money while it compounds into even more money. But they love chronicling flashy wealthy people as they lavishly spend their excess cash – all with the appearance or image that this translates to happiness.

What percentage of the US population do you think that the flashy wealthy types really represent? My guess is that it is small and insignificant, but highly interesting (and greatly magnified) to the media and to people who have never figured out how to quietly grow their own wealth.

And, what percentage of these people will have their fifteen minutes of monetary fame and then burn out financially? More than you might think, unfortunately.

Just because someone is talented enough to make money doesn't mean they will know what to do with it later. Pick your financial role models wisely. Rarely will the media lead you in the right direction.

---

# CHAPTER V

# What the frugal millionaires have to say

The frugal millionaires were asked to freely share ideas in 24 money related categories where they felt they had something to contribute. They were promised strict anonymity in exchange for being forthcoming with their ideas. They did not hold back. They have opinions that have put a lot of money in their pockets (and kept it there).

If they chose to, the comments they provided could be associated with their initials. For many of them their initials were jumbled a bit so that they would know they contributed, but you won't know who they are. The ideas presented are, of course, more important than exactly who said them. The frugal millionaires know this. Others preferred complete anonymity, so you will see references using the initials *AFM*.

*AFM* = Anonymous Frugal Millionaire (and there are many of them).

Some comments may have been edited for clarity and conciseness. As you will see, there are a lot of valuable insights in the pages ahead.

## *How to use this book:*

Pick one of the 24 categories ahead that you are interested in and see what the frugal millionaires have to say about it. If you are considering buying or leasing a car then read how the frugal millionaires do it. If you are wondering how to better handle your credit cards just look at how the frugal millionaires handle theirs. Not sure about what kind of mortgage to get? The frugal millionaires can give you their ideas. Or, if you aren't sure what a good investment strategy could be for you see what the frugal millionaires think. It's like having dozens of millionaires sitting in your living room giving you their honest and direct ideas on just about any topic related to money. Sometimes they agree and sometimes they contradict each other. That just proves there are many ways to grow wealth. Use this book to challenge conventional "wisdom" and debunk urban legends and myths about money. Consider these valuable ideas and use them to your advantage.

After the 24 categories there is a chapter entitled: Creating the *model* frugal millionaire. It represents a fundamental set of best practices that you can embrace to grow your wealth. If you focus on these best practices you can change the way you think about your money and being frugal, and grow your net worth. If you want to read them now go directly to page 173. You can always jump back into the specific category sections that interest you later.

# 1. Financial investments

As you will read, the frugal millionaires are passionate
about many topics. Making sound financial investments is
one of them. They may have many different approaches,
but the end result is the same...they have grown their net
worth and they are telling you how they did it.

*REMINDER: 91.4% of the frugal millionaires have seen
their net worth increase since they became millionaires.
7.1% have seen their net worth stay about the same.
Only 1.4% (one person) saw their net worth decrease
since they had become a millionaire. (And this was
attributed to too many fancy dinners financed by personal credit card debt.) Even the frugal millionaires
aren't perfect!*

## *Philosophies*

*AFM* – First, have a plan! If you are making a risky
investment never invest more than you can truly afford to
lose. If you "go for broke" and take on too much risk you
probably will "go broke."

SLL – Rules of investing in stocks:

> <u>Rule #1</u>: Don't invest in anything you don't
> understand. You are buying a piece of a busi-
> ness, not "betting" on price movement. Read
> books on investing.
> <u>Rule #2</u>: Assess your risk tolerance. What's more
> important, the safety of what you have or growth?
> Pick the longest time horizon. Longer is better.
> <u>Rule #3</u>: Have a good reason to purchase, like
> good management or if the stock is undervalued.

<u>Rule #4</u>: Diversify. Buy funds until you know enough to buy individual stocks. Look for low expense ratios.

J&CB – We have a buy and hold philosophy. Always, always, always invest your windfalls.

JTA – The best advice I can give you is to invest your money or go into a business that pays you when you are awake, sleeping, eating and/or on vacation. Otherwise, start investing early and be patient. Be weary of get rich quick schemes. When everyone was at the water cooler talking about stocks or became a day trader in the late 1990's it should have been a sign to get out of the market. When everyone was a part time speculative home builder in the early 2000's it should have been a sign to get out of that market.

*AFM* – I realized that I would never develop wealth with my wages and that I needed to leverage my wages and take calculated risks with the money I earned. I have noted that many other women are not willing to take on the level of risk I have been willing to take on hence they remain wage slaves.

DMG – Constantly look for ways to increase your rate of return by 1%. It will make a difference.

KJH – Save your money. Don't try to time the market. Have a sound investment strategy.

MG&DG – Be prepared to take some risks. Set aside a portion of your money that may be considered a riskier investment with a higher rate of potential return.

WAL – Invest in what you can see, visit, try or use. Peter Lynch, the original Magellan Fund manager, said that he only invested in companies which he could see first hand or if he used their products because he believed that his personal experience gave him an understanding of how well the company would perform.

B&GH – I never wake up in the middle of the night screaming, "Oh God, I have too much of my money in cash!" Hope for the best but plan for the worst. When your stocks are up 10%, take that money off the table and move it into safer things. Decide how much you are willing to lose and put the rest in safe places. Don't confuse amusements with investments. Cars, boats and planes are amusements.

VTN – I spent a number of years in the hospitality industry, but my paycheck did little other than provide me with seed money for my net worth. I saved a set amount with every paycheck, and more whenever I could. My "wealth" came from conservative, long term investing in the stock market and real estate.

*AFM* – Keep some money aside to invest for yourself, but not the majority. Don't get greedy, take a good return and be happy. Don't get mad or remain upset if you lose. Learn from it. Never risk more than you can afford to lose.

NM&JPR – Compounding is king. Go for long term investments rather than a quick buck.

DLS – Don't "play" the stock market.

*AFM* – Adopt an investment philosophy and never change in response to daily news.

*AFM* – Save or invest at least 25% of your wages.

### Diversification

AA – Diversify above everything else. Make sure your "nest egg" is highly diversified across all financial categories and territories. Then, take your "risk money" and make some bets based on your career experience and market insights. This allows you to be creative and take some upside risk, while never threatening your financial core.

BEH – I break down my investments into three groups:

1) <u>Preservation</u>: Typically municipal bonds. These have paid off nicely and limit downside.
2) <u>Risk</u>: Mix of stocks.
3) <u>Income producing assets</u>: Real estate and cash producing small businesses (laundry mats, car washes, etc.).

RP – Mix high-risk return with conservative low-risk, low-return investments.

JC – Diversify not just the types of investments but the geography and company life stage of your investments. Look for minimum fees. Cut your losses quickly and let the winners run.

*AFM* – Invest in Index Funds, IRA's, 401(k)'s and income producing real estate.

*AFM* – I am a basic investor and always operate on a 30/30/30 and 10 investment model. I invest:

- 30% in solid "old school" investments
- 30% in areas that interest me personally

- 30% in foreign investments and,
- 10% in "what the hell" investments.

ERK – Remember two very important terms because they have real consequences: risk and diversification. Even being conservative sometimes has risk (sometimes CDs don't beat inflation) so you need to know what exposure you have and are comfortable with.

*AFM* – Be balanced in your investments, whatever balanced means to you (more stock when you are young, more bonds when you are older, real estate to diversify). Know what your risk profile is and stick with it...even when the market turns down.

### Financial advisors

*A financial advisor is defined here as someone you partner with to guide your financial destiny. They may be compensated based on a flat fee basis or on an extremely low percentage management fee based on the value of the investments that you hold with them. A stock broker who makes money (commissions) only from buying and selling your stocks is not part of the definition of a financial advisor. (SOURCE: the author)*

*REMINDER: 57% of the frugal millionaires used a financial advisor.*

RJC – Be careful of who you choose as a money manager. Interview them. Challenge them. Talk to their other clients. Find one that is interested in preserving your wealth rather than making themselves wealthy. Diversify your wealth. Don't depend on just the stock market. Read books on investing so you will know what the financial "wonks" are saying.

*AFM* – Always ask what the net worth of your money manager is. If it's not similar to yours, or higher, she/he won't be able to relate to you and your goals.

SR&BS – Find a good financial person and make them tell you how they invest their own money.

JSB – If you love investing and paying close attention to the markets AND you are good at it, go ahead and do it yourself. Otherwise hire a pro.

RME – My financial advisor is my friend. I see them every Wednesday for lunch. They keep me informed. My CPA is also my friend. They keep me in the positive. Work with people you trust.

*AFM* – Don't do it yourself. Get a wealth advisor and have them pick the best portfolio managers. Diversify across domestic equities, international equities, municipals, real estate and hedge funds.

*AFM* – Seek professional advice from a trusted money manager. Make sure that money manager takes time over the years to understand: your values, your financial goals and your tolerance for risk.

*AFM* – Stick with what you know or are interested in, or what your financial advisor knows. Just as in work, if you don't find it interesting you won't care and not paying attention can cost lots of money.

JDS – I'll trade the opportunity cost of personally managed, stress inducing investments for the steady and durable returns of low maintenance professional managers every time.

RDF – Find a good manager and leave your investments alone. You do not know anything. Frankly, they do not know anything either, but they focus on it. Do not pick stocks. If you want to lose money, lose money investing in a restaurant or something you'll enjoy.

FJC – I have had the same advisor for over 12 years and they manage more than 80% of my portfolio. I personally manage the portion of my portfolio that is in the industry where I work.

JMM&DRS – We use a "fee only" financial planner. We have stopped individually investing in stocks so we don't have to spend too much time on financial matters and can enjoy life and work more.

DAS – Take the time to conduct a thorough interview. Seek referrals from friends and trusted colleagues. Choose an appropriate strategy and stick to it...even through the ups and downs. Think as long term as you can afford to.

### Index funds

*DEFINITION: An index fund is a collective investment scenario (usually a mutual fund or an exchange-traded fund) that aims to replicate the movements of an index of a specific financial market. An index fund is created by trying to hold all of the securities in the index, in the same proportions as the index. Many index funds rely on a computer model with little or no human input in the decision as to which securities to purchase and is therefore a form of passive management. The lack of active management (stock picking and market timing) usually gives the advantage of lower fees and lower taxes in taxable accounts. (SOURCE: Fidelity Investments, with edits)*

*EXAMPLE: An S&P 500 Index Fund takes all the stocks in the S&P 500 and buys enough shares in each company to represent the dollar value of that each company represents as a percentage of that market. So, if the Acme Company represented 2% of the value of all the S&P 500 companies combined then an S&P 500 Index Fund would have 2% of its dollar value in Acme stock.*

*Since markets generally (meaning almost always) outperform managed funds, and have significantly lower management fees than managed funds, they are a better investment alternative. This is why the frugal millionaires like them as part of their portfolios. Their success/failure is also easier to track. If the S&P 500 went up 1.5% over a one week period so did your S&P 500 Index Fund. The same would be true if it went down.*

*Index funds are part of a balanced stress-free portfolio. You can use them to buy an overall "market" position. But you should also be considering other options with a portion of your portfolio in more risky investments (only to the degree that you can afford to lose that money) and some conservative options as well. It will all depend on your personal risk profile.*

*AFM* – Index Funds are lower cost and perform better than almost all other similar funds, plus the managed funds have high fees that typically eat into your earnings. Over time that could ruin you. Managed (not indexed) funds that do well often have money rush in and then under perform while new investments are made.

DTA – Use Index Funds, like S&P 500, Russell 1000, Russell 2000, EAFE International Index Funds and Wilshire 5000, etc. No-load and low expense mutual funds would be next on my list.

*AFM* – In nearly every investor letter that Warren Buffett writes he talks about putting your money in Index Funds. Who can argue with that? If you must buy a mutual fund, never buy a "loaded" one (just say no to upfront commissions!).

*AFM* – Buy Index Funds since personal or even broker stock picking falls behind Vanguard or Fidelity Index Funds about 80% of the time. Don't sell them.

*AFM* – Rebalance your portfolio annually and if you don't have the time or interest in doing your homework use a planner or buy index funds.

*In Lehman's Terms:*
## WARREN BUFFETT'S INDEX FUND BET

Would you put your money where Warren Buffet's mouth is? I would. Mr. Buffett, one of the world's wealthiest people, recently made a bet that the average return of the Vanguard S&P 500 Index Fund (net of all fees, costs and expenses) would out perform a hedge fund firm's "hedge fund of funds" (made up of five funds) over the next 10 years. (This raises the obvious question: How many funds could a hedge fund fund if a hedge fund could fund funds? ...Sorry, couldn't resist!)

Each party bet $320,000 and together they bought a zero-coupon Treasury bond that will be worth $1,000,000 in 10 years. The winner will be one of the charities designated by each of the bettors.

In early voting, 79% of the respondents to a *Fortune* poll believe that the S&P 500 Index Fund will win.

## 2. Stock options

Outside of starting a company and owning most of its stock, being an employee and earning stock options is potentially one of the more lucrative ways to create wealth. Options can be complicated (like knowing the difference between qualified and non-qualified options, and the tax issues related to them) but when they have the potential for real monetary value it can be worth the effort to understand them. Some of the frugal millionaires have created their millions with stock options and because of that they offer some very specific ideas on the topic.

FYI: I'm not referring to playing the stock market put/call option game here. In fact, you don't even have to know what those terms mean. They don't apply here and they are not the same thing. What I am talking about is getting stock options as part of your compensation in a company you work for.

*DEFINITION: Stock options from your employer give you the right to buy a specific number of shares of your company's stock during a time and at a price that your employer specifies. (SOURCE: howstuffworks.com)*

*EXAMPLE: You go to work for the Beta Company and get 10,000 options over a four year period. In simplified terms, you would "vest" (earn) 25% of those options at the end of each of those four years. You could then decide to "exercise" (sell) those options (convert them into shares) and take a profit (assuming the options are for shares of stock that have more value than what the option costs you.) Always consult an accountant for tax considerations when exercising options.*

### Philosophies

T&RR – When you are holding a bunch of options/stock in your company that you could sell, but are not, then think about it this way: Assume, for the sake of argument, that you did sell the options/stock and had the cash. Would you take that cash and buy the stock back? If yes, then hold the stock. If not, then get rid of it. Never make taxes a part of this consideration – you've got to pay them sooner or later and tax considerations always cause folks to make the wrong decision.

JSB – Options are way more complicated than most people realize. You must really understand how they work and don't ever count on them materializing.

JDS – In the technology world, this is your compensation. Salary is just noise.

JLL – Always get them if you can. Equity/ownership is the way to financial independence.

AFM – Accumulate as many as you can in private companies as long as they are cheap. Assume they will never be worth anything, but eventually some will.

NM&JPR – They are icing on the cake – but you shouldn't expect to retire on them.

S&AW – Don't fall in love with stock options. They are not a reflection of who you are, they are a financial vehicle – use them as such.

### Strategies

DC – These are just part of your compensation. Evaluate the whole package. If you have a high risk tolerance and can afford to gamble, find a company that is poised to be successful.

DLS – Take more cash instead of options, unless you can afford to gamble.

*AFM* – Treat stock options as "found money," not as part of your core financial plan. Never, never, never take out a margin loan for your options. We never did this thankfully, but had friends in three separate companies lose their shirts.

DAS – Most people focus on strike price (the cost of the option) and vesting schedule for options. Don't forget to negotiate acceleration (more options if the company goes public or is acquired) and expiration (how long the options are good for) as well.

*AFM* – Cash or stock options? TAKE THE CASH!

*AFM* – Don't gamble your house down-payment savings on exercising options.

## When to exercise or sell them

*AFM* – If you exercise early and enough time has gone by you will only pay capital gains. When it's time to exercise them into shares sell 1/3 for taxes, sell 1/3 to diversify, and keep the remaining 1/3 or sell it all and invest somewhere else.

SR&BS – Sell them when they vest. Do not be greedy. Ever. Not even once.

FJC – If you own stock options and there is a liquidity event, sell whatever you can whenever you can and invest the return using a good financial advisor. Don't get fancy and wait to "time" the sale in the market for maximum stock price. Sell, Sell, Sell.

*AFM* – Exercise most immediately and keep a small amount for possible upside.

ERK – Don't get greedy on these. Remember: 50% of a lot is much more than 100% of nothing. Options are always risky and their value is not guaranteed to go up.

MG&DG – If your net worth is heavily based on one company sell at least 50% of your stock options once you are in long term gain range and invest in 2-4 funds that are diversified.

B&GH – Once there's a public market for your stock, put yourself on a programmed selling routine every quarter. Sell the same amount each quarter regardless of the current price. Hang on to 1/3 of the total in case your ship comes in. By locking in the selling plan you're less likely to hold too much of your own company stock – something you would never do if you were just planning a balanced portfolio among all your assets.

*AFM* – Only do an early exercise of options if the strike price and the stock price are very low at the time of exercise (under $1), AND only if you have the money to lose. If you do exercise early consult a CPA for the tax ramifications.

*DEFINITION: A strike price is the value of an option on the day it is granted to an employee.*

*AFM* – Sell them on a regular basis. There are too many of us who have held on too long and paid the price.

BEH – Sell them as soon as they vest.

### *Tax implications*

SLL – Exercise them as early as possible to minimize taxes. Sell the stock if you think it's over priced. Hold it if you think it's under priced.

*AFM* – Early exercise if you can. You will save a lot in taxes.

RJC – Exercise early and get your critical long term holding period out of the way. Remember that there can be an Alternative Minimum Tax (AMT) problem and always evaluate what the impact of that could be. If the company is a dud don't bother early exercising.

*NOTE: The definition of AMT (Alternative Minimum Tax) is found on page 121.*

B&GH – File your 83b forms right away to start the tax clock ticking for capital gains. We're not likely to see capital gains taxes this low again for a long time.

*DEFINITION: Section 83b Election: A tax filing with the IRS within 30 days of grant that allows employees granted stock to pay taxes on the grant date instead of on the date restrictions lapse. If an employee files the election, taxes are based on the fair market value on the grant date, with any future appreciation taxed as a capital gain. If the employee does not file an election, taxes are based on the fair market value on the date the restrictions lapse, which will be higher assuming that the stock has appreciated in value. (SOURCE: MoneyGlossary.com, with edits)*

AD – Donate appreciated options to charity for tax mitigation.

*AFM* – Depending on the type of option you are exercising (NSO or ISO) make sure you exercise early so you minimize your taxes. This is confusing stuff, talk to your accountant.

*DEFINITION: Non-Qualified Stock Option (NSO) – Nonqualified stock options are a popular form of equity compensation. Companies like them because they provide a flexible and efficient way to attract, retain and motivate employees (and other service providers, such as directors and consultants). Employees like them because they represent an opportunity to grow wealth, with tax consequences deferred until the year of exercise.*

*Nonqualified options have two disadvantages compared to incentive stock options. One is that you have to report taxable income at the time you exercise the option to buy stock, and the other is that the income is treated as compensation, which is taxed at higher rates than long-term capital gains. (SOURCE: Fairmark.com)*

*DEFINITION: Incentive Stock Option (ISO) – Incentive stock options (ISOs) are a form of equity compensation that provides unique tax benefits – and significant tax complexity. In recent years their popularity has grown to roughly match the popularity of nonqualified stock options.*

*Incentive stock options provide a way to avoid both of the disadvantages of NSOs. There's no income to report at the time you exercise the option (unless you sell the stock at the same time you buy it). And if you hold the stock long enough to satisfy a special holding period, your gain from the stock will be treated as long-term capital gain. These tax advantages are partly offset by the Alternative Minimum Tax (AMT). (SOURCE: Fairmark.com)*

A word on a new kind of stock option: The Restricted Stock Unit (RSU). These have become popular because companies are now required to expense employee stock options.

*DEFINITION: A Restricted Stock Unit (RSU) is a grant valued in terms of company stock, but company stock is not issued at the time of the grant. After the recipient of a unit satisfies the vesting requirement, the company distributes shares, or the cash equivalent of the number of shares used to value the unit. Depending on plan rules, the participant or donor may be allowed to choose whether to settle in stock or cash.*

*Once an employee is granted Restricted Stock Units, the employee must decide whether to accept or decline the grant. If the employee accepts the grant, he may be required to pay the employer a purchase price for the grant.*

*After accepting a grant and providing payment (if applicable), the employee must wait until the grant vests.*

*Vesting periods for Restricted Stock Units may be time-based (a stated period from the grant date) or perform-ance-based (often tied to achievement of corporate goals).* (SOURCE: Fidelity Investments, Fidelity.com)

Always consult your tax advisor regarding the tax consequences of stock options.

## 3. Mortgages

Mortgages are a fact of life for most of us, even the frugal millionaires. Their approach to mortgage debt is a bit different depending on their financial goals. "Good" debt in your early years may help you, but over the long term it's best to minimize your exposure to mortgages. There are many ways to pay off your home early. You can then do other smart things with the money that you would have been putting towards a mortgage payment. Some frugal millionaires like mortgages and others don't. The fact is that we will all probably have them at some point in our lives. This section is about the best ways to approach mortgages.

### *Strategies*

*AFM* – Don't be a slave to your mortgage. Don't believe real estate agents, loan officers and seemingly "rich" people when they say that you should "stretch and buy big." Your home and mortgage should reflect what your goals are. My goals involve family and freedom. That means that I wanted a house that was nice, big enough for a family, etc....but not so expensive that both my wife and I would have to work –or– that I would have to work in such a time-suck job that I'd never be home. Where's the freedom in that scenario? The result: my wife has never had to work, we've never been late on a payment or had to dip into investments. Why? Because we were never over-extended in the first place. That has kept our wealth growing and our sanity and freedom intact.

SLL – Compare deals and rates online. Don't pay points. Scrutinize fees. Watch the bond and mortgage rates to see where the trends might be going. Don't sign anything until you lock in a rate.

*AFM* – If you can't truly afford to buy something then don't buy it yet. Whatever the real estate and mortgage people say you can afford you will always be better off spending a lot less. Don't become house poor or house stupid.

RJC – Be reasonable and don't buy over your head. Yeah, you can buy a really expensive home, but eventually the maintenance and taxes will eat you up. I went for a nice but modest home that we could easily afford.

MG&DG – Spend less than what you qualify for.

*AFM* – Before you even get a mortgage make sure your credit is in great shape and you know exactly what your credit scores are (all three of them). You will be in a better negotiation position on interest rates.

S&AW – Don't buy the biggest house you can "afford." Buy a house that won't be viewed as a financial burden. Nothing makes you less mobile than a mortgage you can't fund.

*AFM* – You can only afford a house when your income, after taxes and expenses, allows you to: 1) Save for your children's education, 2) Save for your future, and 3) save for short term needs.

R&DW – Don't get emotionally attached to your primary residence and you will be able to take advantage of the opportunity to pay zero capital gains taxes on the first $500K of profit (if you are married, or $250K for individuals) on your primary residence every two years.

*AFM* – Think about this: What would your target house price and mortgage be if you/your spouse went from two incomes down to one...or your income fell by half? Buy a mortgage and a home accordingly and you'll own the bank, the bank won't own you.

*AFM* – Look at what you mortgage really costs you in interest charges over time. You might also think twice before financing all your closing costs...since you will be paying for them for 15-30 years too. Read the paperwork and look at all the fees. They are often negotiable.

MW – Refinance to get a lower rate, not to pull equity out.

ERK – Pay attention the first time you go through this because you will likely buy/sell property many times and you need to understand the steps in the process, your options, your commitments and what you are signing.

*AFM* – Don't use a home equity line of credit to pay off a credit card or buy a car...that's not leverage...you will pay interest on it for decades.

*AFM* – Make the mortgage decision based on whether it helps you financially for a reasonable amount of risk, and NOT out of principle (for example: I don't want to have a mortgage because "my parents always complained about the mortgage payment so I swore I would never have one").

### Mortgage length and type

*AFM* – Stick with a 15 or 30 year conventional loan. Don't go for the tricky ARMs (Adjustable Rate Mortgages) or interest only deals...you won't like it when they adjust or if/when the real estate market goes down.

AA – Never mortgage more than 50% of your property. Go for fixed rate loans over 30 years and try to pay it off in 15. The adjustable rate mortgages are too unpredictable, despite their initial appeal. If it's worth investing in a property, then it's worth paying a fixed rate and making the commitment to hold through at least one real estate cycle.

JLL – 15 year, fixed mortgages are the only way to go!

RJC – If the money is cheap it can be smart to arbitrage the cost of the mortgage vs. the benefits of tax deductions and market gains. We actually locked in a 15 year mortgage and put enough cash aside for two years of payments because we could earn a higher interest rate than our mortgage. The money I would have used to pay cash for part of the house was earning a much higher interest rate so we didn't want to touch it.

*AFM* – Stick with standard fixed rate structures, they are cheaper. Rates and costs are the only thing that matter, not the monthly payment amounts.

WCA – If there is money in the family and everyone is on good terms, then borrowing from the family makes a ton of sense. (As long as it's well documented, at current rates, and viewed in a business like fashion by all participants.)

## Reducing your mortgage

*AFM* – Make a half payment every two weeks. You will pay your mortgage off years sooner and not waste a bunch of money on interest charges. There are mortgage pay down calculators online to show you how this works.

NM&JPR – Take opportunities to pay off a little of the capital on your mortgage whenever you can – even if it seems like an insignificant amount. The compound interest saved over the lifetime of the mortgage is much larger.

*AFM* – Mortgages lose their interest rate deduction efficiency the older they get. This means that you are paying more principle towards the end of the loan. Pay them off as soon as you can.

JKB – Always pay 20% more on your monthly payment.

## Those "for" mortgages

*AFM* – Mortgages make sense if there is a tax advantage when compared to what you are paying in interest over a long period of time. They are better when you are younger and have less money upfront. Over time the amount of interest becomes less and the amount of principle becomes higher as a percentage of your payment....so you slowly lose the value of the deduction. Most people don't know this.

WAL – The US Government tax system is set up to reward those who have mortgages. Whether you're a renter or have your house paid off, you're taking advantage of our government's benevolence.

*AFM* – If you have a high value property that has enormous equity already, get an interest only loan. It's less expensive in the long run and if you put the money aside that you would have spent on a conventional mortgage you will get interest on that and pay off the mortgage faster.

JTA – When it comes to residences, mortgages can be a way for someone to save cash for investing and therefore possibly allow them to earn a higher rate of investment return than one is paying in mortgage interest.

RDF – If the government is going to pay you to own a home, why turn them down?

JT&B – If you can have money at a cheap rate then a mortgage is a great decision. Always have a 6-12 month reserve (savings account, money market fund, etc.) to pay your mortgage and pay into it regularly.

### *Those "against" mortgages*

JSB – If you want absolute piece of mind, don't have any debt. But, with mortgage rates often being so low and other investments with nice ROIs (Return On Investment), a certain amount of mortgage debt might make sense. A mortgage with a balloon payment is likely akin to suicide (sub-prime anyone?).

KJH – Stay out of debt.

*AFM* – For many people the advantage of the "interest deduction" is a myth perpetuated by real estate agents, mortgage brokers and even your friends. Have you ever looked at how much you pay in interest charges over the life of a loan? Having the smallest mortgage possible and investing what you would have been paying in interest can be better in the long run, even if you do have to pay some taxes.

JTA – I prefer not to have one and say get rid of them as fast as you can. Debt will kill you.

B&GH – There's a great feeling living in a home that you own outright.

AFM – This is a personal choice. If you really don't need to have one then don't do it. I personally think you can do other things with your money than have it tied-up in your main residence.

DTA – Play it conservative. Don't take on a lot of debt. Be debt free – including mortgages.

DAS – Don't over extend.

JMM&DRS – We don't intend to have a mortgage in retirement. We only have a mortgage to maximize tax benefits.

### *In Lehman's Terms:*
## YOUR HOME IS A FORCED SAVINGS PLAN?

Calling your home a "forced savings plan" as some people do makes no true financial sense. This seems like an urban myth that keeps perpetuating itself. What most people think this means is that by having a mortgage you are creating a forced savings account by making your mortgage payments. Otherwise you might blow the money on something else. This theory is often based on the assumption that there will be an increase in value of your home over time. But is this really a savings plan? No, not really.

Why? In a savings account the money goes in and you'll get some token interest rate for it. And it is protected. With your mortgage you pay taxes and interest on your home, you possibly get a small year over year return (and that's in some markets…if your home goes up in value at all – there are no guarantees), and you have to pay fees and interest to the bank if you ever want to take any home equity money out. You also have to pay a bundle in commissions and other costs to sell the home at the end of its useful life. There is also home maintenance to consider.

Does that sound like a good "forced savings plan" to you?

Take a home for what it is: a place to live that might have some tax advantages and some equity in the future. If you want a real savings plan then open one up at a bank or a credit union.

## 4. Real estate

Real estate is one of the many paths that the frugal millionaires have taken to grow their wealth. Simply investing in real estate does not guarantee success however. Some swear by real estate, some swear at it. It's what you invest in and how you do it that makes the difference. The frugal millionaires have plenty of thoughts on the subject.

*Buying strategies*

*AFM* – I invested in real estate because I could understand it unlike the stock market which was and remains incomprehensible to me.

*AFM* – Real estate can be a great way to make money over time, but limit how much you invest.

*AFM* – I prefer to keep my life simple. Real estate is a good investment but adds stress and complication unless you can afford a management company, or you have time to work on the property management issues.

RME – I purchased my own office building, my home and a condo for each child while they are in college. Real estate eventually appreciates and I would rather have the security of ownership for my family than renting. Invest in the condo markets around universities. There will always be housing demand.

*AFM* – They aren't making more land!

JMM&DRS – We invest in real estate LLCs and REITs.

*DEFINITIONS: Limited Liability Company (LLC): A business ownership structure that offers its owners the advantage of limited liability (like corporations) and partnership-like taxation, in which profits are passed through to the owners and taxed on their personal income tax returns. (SOURCE: Nolo Press, Nolo.com)*

*NOTE: LLCs are not limited to real estate investments only, but in this case they are created as a way to minimize risk when a group of people want to invest in some type of real estate. It could be a house, apartments, condos, land...pretty much anything.*

*DEFINITION: Real Estate Investment Trust (REIT): A security that sells like a stock on the major exchanges and invests in real estate directly, either through properties or mortgages. They receive special tax considerations, and typically offer investors high yields as well as a highly liquid method of investing in real estate. Individuals can either invest in REITs by purchasing their shares directly on an open exchange or by investing in a mutual fund that specializes in public real estate. (SOURCE: Financial Dictionary, freedictionary.com)*

DES – With real estate you can learn the power of leveraging your money. You can grow your net worth and save on taxes.

VTN – My best investments have been in real estate.

AFM – Real estate continues to be a good investment, always buy where there is sustainable income. Rarely can real estate speculation pay off in resort areas – witness some of the valuations today.

## Primary homes

S&AW – If you believe in the idea of a broad portfolio – it is likely that your first home will offer you plenty of real estate exposure, especially if you are young.

AFM – Keep your "investment" in your primary home minimal. Don't buy a McMansion. You won't have money to invest in other things that will be important.

BEH – My home is my castle and there is no need for another one, unless it is income producing.

SLL – Better to buy a shabby house in a great neighborhood than the other way around.

T&RR – I do not consider housing an investment. It is a luxury for me and my family – a place to customize and call home.

## Second homes – some say yes

JSB – Think about it before you do it. If you love houses and love renovating, building on and taking care of them then go ahead. But, you can rent a hell of a place every year of your life for what you will pour into a second home.

AFM – Only buy a second home if it is income producing. Be careful about the owner usage rules and the tax codes. Only buy any additional real estate if it's income producing. Have someone else pay the bills on it while it's appreciating.

DES – You should only have a second home if you can pay it off or rent it out to cover the payment.

ERK – Up until the last few years I would say you couldn't go wrong with a second home. The key thing is to make sure you don't over extend yourself just to have one.

*AFM* – If we did buy a vacation property it would be no further than a two hour drive from our home.

*AFM* – Buy a second home only if you can: 1) afford it, 2) rent it while not being used, and 3) if you are going to spend the same amount of time in it as your first home.

NM&JPR – If it is a holiday home some distance away, the most important question to ask yourself is: "Who is going to look after it in our absence?"

*AFM* – Owning a second home should be a pleasure, not a chore. Buy it only if you intend to use it or retire in it.

*AFM* – Only buy a second home if you truly have the excess money and can afford to not use it if you don't want.

DTA – I understand real estate and the area where I bought has been appreciating. I rent it when I'm not there. I plan to transition to this home in retirement.

JTA – Only buy a second home in areas with huge barriers to growth like beach front properties.

AA – Buying a second home is great for the soul, but remember that appreciation of the asset could be very slow over time and you are taking money out of your portfolio that would be appreciating with the market.

## Second homes – some say no

*AFM* – When the economy drops second homes are the first to go.

B&GH – Don't confuse real estate investments with second homes. If you need and want a second home to live in from time to time, do that. If you want to make money in real estate, look into REITs and other related instruments.

WCA – Second homes are hard to justify as investments. You might catch an upwardly moving market, but associated costs generally eat up appreciation.

*AFM* – Second homes are rarely good investments. Only do this if you have a sufficient nest egg outside of it.

BEH – I do not have a second home and likely will not. There are too many other places to go for me to be interested in a weekend retreat.

JDS – Homes can own you as much as you own them. If you lead a busy life it's hard to make a second home work.

*AFM* – A second home is never the right decision financially. It always costs more than staying in hotels and makes you feel obligated to go to the second home even if you'd rather vacation elsewhere.

*AFM* – Second homes are expenses, not investments. The "profit" you make will only lessen the total expense.

JMM&DRS – NO, NO, NO to a second home. We believe you can pay for A LOT of rentals hotels in amazing places around the world for what you spend on a second place.

We don't want the extra work associated with a second place or with real estate investments.

TR&R – Second, third and fourth homes are even less of an investment and more of a luxury.

### *Investment property*

RJC – Always view real estate as an investment that might need to be sold if the price is right. I find that renting homes is a better deal then buying a second home.

R&DW – Only buy as an investment based on growth potential or for rentals, not because you become enamored with an area and think you will spend a good amount of time there. Tax advantages are on a second home only, so don't go beyond.

JTA – I believe real estate is one of the safest long term investments and for someone who truly knows what they are doing it can make you wealthy very fast.

AFM – When investing in property – DO NOT go in with friends and family. It never goes well.

MG&DG – Invest in something that isn't reliant on renters. Buy property that has low annual expenses and can sit and increase in value until you are ready to sell it.

AFM – Income producing real estate is a good addition to a diversified investment portfolio.

WAL – Don't buy a second home, buy income producing property.

JC – Consider raw property outside of the home. Think about international diversification.

*AFM* – Real estate investments are a great part of a diversified portfolio, but REITs, land or even timber companies will give you fewer headaches than vacation properties or adding "Landlord" to your title. We don't own a second home because we'd rather use the money to explore our planet.

*AFM* – Buy commercial real estate if you have a secure, long-term tenant and a good property manager.

JT&B – We do a real estate fund and like to rent vacation places as of now.

## *In Lehman's Terms:*
## REAL ESTATE MARKETING

In a recent ad campaign for the National Association of Realtors,® the voice-over talent says that "60% of the average homeowner's wealth is from their home's equity."

Let's think about that for a minute. Has any financial advisor ever told you to put 60% of your investments all in one place? Hopefully not! Fire them if they ever do. As we've seen in the recent past, home values can go down, dramatically, and send the financial markets into a tailspin.

People living in $1 million dollar homes that used to be worth $1.2 million don't necessarily feel like millionaires these days...and when you subtract out their debt load, they truly aren't!

Of course, if you want access to any of the equity you might have built up in your home you can always go to the bank and borrow against it...and pay a bunch of fees to rent back your own money and do something else with it. (Buying cars and paying off credit cards is not a good idea though.) The downside is that you will be paying thousands of dollars in interest and taxes over the life of that loan to get the value back out of your own home.

Does that sound like a good deal to you?

*In Lehman's Terms:*
## SMART REAL ESTATE SPENDING

One husband and wife frugal millionaire team learned to stick with their instincts when it came to buying their first house.

According to them, back when they bought their home it seemed that every idiot in the market was willing to overbid by 30% to get what was already an expensive home.

The frugal millionaire dynamic duo concluded: 1) They weren't going to give any homeowner any extra profit on what was already an insane profit, 2) They weren't going to line the pockets of any real estate agent or lender, 3) They weren't going to be suckers, and 4) They weren't going to over bid, even by $1 over an asking price.

Their real estate agent did what they told him to do. And the result was? They bought their home in 1999, in the San Francisco Bay area, for asking price. This was unheard of at the time. Their patience paid off.

Just think about how they've invested all the money they didn't have to spend overpaying for their house.

## 5. Buying / leasing / servicing a car

Next to a place to live, a car is, of course, one of the biggest expenses you can have. The frugal millionaires have found ways to drive what they want (within reason) and do it cost effectively. Buying is their primary (and most would say only) choice. Leasing is rarely an option. But there are even more ideas than just those, as you are about to read.

### Strategies

JLL – Always pay cash. Always buy the car with the least options and the smallest engine. It will significantly reduce your depreciation costs which, until the recent surge in gas prices, were the highest cost component to owning an automobile. Wait until the end of the month and negotiate like hell. To save even more money buy higher deductible car insurance.

SLL – The best used deals are at dealers that don't sell that particular brand. If you are buying from a dealer with the brand you want keep nitpicking the car to death and asking for more concessions. Use online websites to find local cars and price ranges. Get service records from the local dealer (they are usually in their global computer system). Check consumer and enthusiast sites for car problem info or repair hints. Check for recall information.

AFM – Buy a car that can last a long time past the payments and still be practical and stylish. I buy used with about 30K-40K miles on the car. I don't like the newest models since they tend to have bugs and be in the shop more.

AFM – Don't finance! With zero percent financing you still have to pay for the depreciation of a new car compared to buying used. Used is more cost effective and used cars these days are well made and durable.

RJC – If you can live with the same car for numerous years (7-10) pay cash and negotiate a long-term warranty. If there is cheap financing (less than 2.9%) then go for it. Finance if it gets you a better deal on the car. (Dealers make a lot of money on this.) Pay off the loan early. The old "cash buyers save money" statement is a myth now.

*AFM* – Buy a car that makes you happy and matches your goals. If you have the money – buy it for cash. Treat it well, service it, invest in it. The car I bought 8 years ago is in excellent shape. In about a year I plan to invest in getting the engine rebuilt so I can get another 100,000 miles out of it. If I hadn't taken care of it I'd be making another $35K "investment" instead of one about 1/6th of that.

RDF – Don't waste money on cars if you don't have any money. Buy a safe (but not cheap) car and focus on enjoying other parts of your life.

*AFM* – Cars with "pre-owned" status and extended factory warranties (included in the price, not the optional versions) often have better warranties than a new car.

JMM&DRS – We have one nice car and one basic car, but no "fancy" sports cars. We do lease one car and expense it in my business. Husband's car is 14 years old and we call it the "dogmobile" because he could care less about it aside from the fact that it runs and is reliable.

*AFM* – Let some other sucker eat the depreciation on a new car. Don't buy the stories that new car dealers tell about used cars being someone else's prior nightmare, they sell those too...you know? And they make a lot of money on them!

## *Buying*

WAL – Buying a lease-return vehicle is the best purchase. If you are fortunate you can find a car with some warranty still on it. Plus, you can buy a luxury vehicle at a realistic price, which the original owner took the depreciation hit on.

WCA – Keep the rig until it is not reasonably serviceable. They lose money from day one, new or used.

R&DW – Buy nearly-new if it's a widely available car to avoid the loss of value.

B&GH – Buy your cars outright. Financing never makes sense.

JTA – I buy cars because I keep them for 5-6 years and take care of them. Buy a warranty.

*AFM* – Unless you have too much money or the desire for cars as "toys," buy stylish but reliable, gently used cars (1-3 years old).

JT&B – Buy last year's model and shop around. Negotiate and don't be afraid to walk out of the dealership.

NM&JPR – Buy within your means. It's not good to use leasing to afford a bigger, better, faster car.

MW – I have always paid cash for my cars for the last 10 years, even before I was a millionaire.

BEH – I buy my vehicles and keep them for a long time. My family and I have three vehicles (one is 8 years old, one is 4 and one is 1). My only car payment has 1.9% financing so I make more money keeping my extra cash invested.

JC – Buy 2-3 year old cars. Sell them after an additional 3-4 years. Get an extended warranty.

VTN – I bought my first car new, and I have always bought used luxury cars since.

AA – It's better to own a car, even though it is a depreciating asset. You pay high transaction costs to enter and exit leases. Try to hold a car at least seven years. Buy quality.

*AFM* – Keeping costs down is all about how long you keep the car. You'll keep it longer if you own it.

### *Leasing*

DMG – Never lease a car.

*AFM* – If you are considering leasing a car someone should come to your house and knock some sense into you. If you do lease anyway, read the lease papers before you sign them and know what will happen if you turn the car in with more miles than you leased it for. Also, watch the wear and tear and damage on a lease car as you will be at the dealer's mercy when you turn it in.

B&GH – Lease only when you can deduct almost all the miles legitimately for business.

*AFM* – If you *have* to lease a car, never lease one for longer than the warranty.

DES – When leasing a car always negotiate the best price possible as that will affect the lease payment.

JSB – If you have a business that you can put the car expense under then lease it (if you must). Otherwise just pay cash (or look for some sweetheart financing deals).

*AFM* – Don't be a victim of low lease rate "come-on" advertising. Those thousands of dollars required at the time of the lease signing is actually subsidizing your monthly payments...and you won't even own the car at the end of the lease. Dumb.

R&DW – If you are already rich, lease only when it is your fun car that you will not purchase and do not want to keep longer than a couple of years.

*AFM* – Leases are not a good idea. You will overpay overall if you do less miles than the lease is for and overpay in extra mileage charges if you put on too many miles. No matter what, you will always get screwed!

*AFM* – Car leases don't make financial sense. Never have. And some car makers are no longer offering them – only because *they* are now the ones getting ripped-off on the residual values of the vehicle after the lease is over.

### Service

*AFM* – Service them regularly and keep them.

*AFM* – Only get your car worked on at the dealer while it's under warranty or if the car requires special tools that independent dealers can't get. Regular service that is done elsewhere in a timely/less expensive fashion should not affect your warranty as long as it is documented.

RME – I buy BMWs with the service included over the life of the regular warranty.

B&GH – Changing the oil every 3,000 miles only makes Jiffy Lube happy. Most modern motor oils are designed to give you 10,000 miles between oil changes.

*AFM* – Ask around for who has the best independent car services in your area and use them. Dealers charge too much, but some give loaners and wash your car for you. Weigh the merits of that into your decision.

*In Lehman's Terms:*
## BRILLIANT CAR BUYING

One frugal millionaire decided to reward his wife and himself with a new Porsche Turbo.

(*Please note: This was done after they made their millions!*).

He quickly determined that watching this shiny new autobahn burner depreciate in the driveway made him mad! So he sold it and bought an older classic 1959 Porsche convertible that is appreciating in value and more fun (and cheaper) to own.

Few cars appreciate, and you have to be careful, but in this case a well thought out "fun" car investment strategy has worked well.

*In Lehman's Terms:*
## RESOURCEFUL CAR PART BUYING

When it's time for service and replacement parts most of us just pay the repair shop whatever the price is. What you might not know is that the "list" prices that some dealers charge for parts are actually set by the dealer, not the manufacturer. And the numbers aren't pretty.

In smaller (meaning less competitive) geographical markets, dealers can charge more because they can get away with it…or so they think.

Sometimes the differences are dramatic. For example: The parts required to do a front brake job on one frugal millionaire's sports car were $700 from a local dealer and $400 from a dealer just 150 miles away. That doesn't seem right does it? All it took was a 15 minute phone call to save $300. "I don't have the time to deal with it" is not an excuse!

You don't know that you are getting taken advantage of unless you do the research for yourself. Many dealers have a higher "local" price and a much lower "out of state or wholesale" price to lure in incremental business. It's better to be one of those "incremental" customers.

This particular frugal millionaire now has relationships with a few different dealers in a thousand mile radius from his home and buys his parts more cost effectively, even when you consider taxes and shipping. It all adds up.

# 6. Credit cards

Credit cards can be good or evil, it all depends on how you use them. For some, credit cards are money wasting conveniences. The frugal millionaires know the right way to use their cards. Many of them have grown their wealth dramatically by not having credit card obligations.

Many people would draw the conclusion that "of course they don't have credit card problems – they're rich!" But in all truth, most of the frugal millionaires came from middle class and sometimes even from poor backgrounds. They view credit the other way around...as a rarely used luxury, not a necessity. These frugal millionaires were living well within their means long before they became wealthy...and they continue to do so and be careful with their credit at the same time.

### Strategies

ERK – For some people these are the most dangerous financial product known to man. They can take a big salary and make it seem like you have nothing in the bank. If you use credit cards a lot, try going for one month spending only cash. You'll see how much above your means you tend to live. It's healthy to learn what you do wrong.

BG&H – There's no reason to try to impress anyone with a gold, platinum, black or plutonium card. The only people who will appreciate this is the credit card company collecting the annual fees.

*AFM* – Pay them off every month. Prepay big purchases the day you get them. Try paying them a little early so you don't run the risk of getting hit with a finance charge or a late fee.

*AFM* – Use the card for short term "float." Think of the card as if you were pulling actual cash out of your wallet.

*DEFINITION: Float is the amount of time you have between making the purchase and when the credit card bill is due. You get "free" short term financing if you pay off the card before it is due. (SOURCE: the author)*

RJC – Use AMEX. It's due every month. It forces you to watch what you spend.

DLS – Don't charge unless you know precisely where the money to pay the bill is going to come from and have the discipline to follow through on payment.

## Perks

*AFM* – Get a "miles" card. Use your miles for longer distance (= more expensive) travel.

B&GH – Get a cash-back card with no annual fee. Mileage cards often pay you less than cash-back cards.

J&CB – Get the cards with miles and points, never carry a balance and use the points and miles for Christmas gifts.

SLL – Get a "no fee" card with rewards like cash or mileage.

AD – Go for hotel points.

T&RR – Amex Platinum is worth the big money per year and more than pays for itself with the hotel amenities.

VNN – Pay no fees. Use a dividend card. Redeem your earned cash as frequently as possible and put it into an interest bearing account.

## Monthly credit card balances and interest payments

*AFM* – If you can't afford to pay off the balance each month then you probably shouldn't buy on credit. If you believe you have the self control to buy on credit, make sure you set specific limits on your credit and don't exceed them. If you over extend yourself you can end up with credit card balances that you will be paying off for the rest of your life.

JSB – Don't ever carry credit card debt! This is purely a "math idiot" tax on the stupid and undisciplined.

*AFM* – Pay them off every month or burn them.

SR&BS – Don't ever, ever carry a balance. Plain old dumb.

R&DW – Use a credit card to float dollars and for perks, but never pay interest.

RDF – Worst kind of debt you can have.

VTN – I pay mine off 100% every month. Have been doing so since I was 25 and found out then that holding a balance would put me in the poor house.

## Number of cards

*AFM* – Get one card with a big credit limit. Use only a small portion of the credit limit and it will improve your credit score.

WAL – It's good to have one credit card. Multiple credit cards are silly and add complexity to your personal finances.

*AFM* – Only have one or two credit cards.

S&AW – Have one of each major type: American Express, Visa and MasterCard. Do most of your spending on one so you can track it easily.

DTA – Have three cards, one for business and two for personal. Use the perks. Use the cards to track and analyze your expenses.

*In Lehman's Terms:*
## I WANT IT ALL, AND I WANT IT NOW!

Chase Bank recently ran a credit card ad campaign called "I want it all, and I want it now."

You can probably already guess where I'm going with this...!

The commercial portrayed a male cardholder checking on his cell phone to see if he had enough credit left to get that big TV he always wanted (once the woman in his life said, "You're right, we need a new TV!"). The campaign tagline was "Chase What Matters."

Sure, an HDTV is what really matters! Were they kidding? No. The message was that you could check your balances from your cell phone, but the implied message was: sure, go out and buy whatever stuff you want because you have the credit. Of course you will have to bear the brunt of it later, when your credit card bills come in. But that wouldn't make for an entertaining TV commercial, would it?

Chase and their ad agency caught a lot of rightly deserved grief for that campaign on the consumer finance blogs. They should have.

As my Mom and Dad have always said, "Everything is good...in moderation." If only some of the credit card companies promoted *that* concept.

## 7. Eating at home / eating out / entertainment

We all have to eat. How we do that determines how much money we have in the bank at the end of the month. The only frugal millionaire who didn't see their net worth increase since becoming a millionaire attributed that to too many meals out that were financed on a personal credit card.

One media misperception of millionaires is that they have drinks and eat out all the time, at the finest bars and restaurants. You aren't vibrant and alive if you aren't out hitting the town...right? Nope. As noted earlier, only one out of the 70 frugal millionaires succumbed to this life-style and that does not make a trend for this group. Most of the frugal millionaires take a different approach to eating and entertaining...and they aren't any less "alive" because of it.

### *Eating at home*

NM&JPR – If you have a lovely kitchen at home, use it! Entertaining at home can be more fun than eating out all the time. Dining out is special, so keep it that way.

*AFM* – I go to the best bakery in town and buy their day old bread...and freeze it. I also cook at home. It's better for you, costs less, and you can linger as long as you like. You can invite a lot of people over and have them bring parts of the meal. It's the experience that matters.

SLL – The most efficient breakfast food is oatmeal. (!)

*AFM* – The food and wine is better at home – and you'll never get a DUI.

*NOTE: DUI is an acronym for Driving Under the Influence. It is also known as DWI or Driving While Intoxicated. Regardless of what it's called in your state it is NEVER a good idea to drive while even slightly intoxicated.*

*AFM* – Learn to cook at home. It's fun, healthy and saves money. Eating out is fun too…so if you cook at home at least five nights a week you can go out the other two and still not be blowing a bunch of money.

J&CB – We save a lot of money by eating at home. We buy good food and wine and dine well but it cuts the cost of dining out in half, and we usually have more fun.

*AFM* – When we eat at home we aren't picky. Whatever meat is on sale at the market is what we buy. We enjoy being creative in how we prepare it.

*AFM* – Don't eat at restaurants just to avoid cooking.

KJH – After years of traveling for business, I find eating a nice home cooked meal with the family is better than dining out.

*AFM* – Only eat quality, healthy food. Make this a conscious expenditure of money.

DES – Always use coupons when you can.

*AFM* – Have your kids make dinner for the family one day a week during the summer. They learn how to cook on a budget and you get a break.

MJM – I do all three (eating out, dining in and entertaining) but prefer my BBQ at home with friends and family.

JTA – I think one of the greatest joys in life, and one of the best things you can do for your family, is sit down and have dinner together every night, or at least 5 nights a week. I can cook better steak and make a better meal than 90% of the places I would dine out at.

*AFM* – If you have kids at home make sure that you have several "family meals" at home every week.

WCA – We eat at home a lot more than out. Enjoy going out on occasion, but look at what it costs and think about how long the enjoyment really lasts.

### *Eating out*

DMG – Don't order any part of the meal out of habit that doesn't bring you joy. I almost always order water to drink because the beverage is really not important. And it's cheaper.

*AFM* – Eating out is expensive when the point is often to just socialize.

RJC – Eating out is a splurge.

*AFM* – Take home half of what you order and have it the next day. It's like getting a 2:1 dinner deal. Plus you don't gain weight.

JLL – Dining out is a money pit! Order beer.

*AFM* – Stop buying coffee and a pastry in the morning. You'll drop $120 a month or nearly $1500 a year on this habit.

JKB – Treat yourself on occasion by eating out. Have a date night with your spouse but never more than once a week, if it's on your dime.

*AFM* – Eating out is the fastest way to burn cash and not feel like you got anything for it. Go out for stuff you don't know how to cook.

ERK – We eat out WAY too much and our credit cards show it. And when we eat at home we always buy the same day and end up paying a premium. I would plan a week ahead, buy ingredients to use at home and not shop/spend on dinner every day.

KJH – I dine out more out of necessity when I'm away from home or don't have time to cook. Occasionally, we'll go out for dinner at a nice moderately priced restaurant for a change of pace. I generally prefer small local restaurants to the chains.

RME – I tend to eat out close to my office to meet more potential customers. Eventually they find out what I do and become a client. The lunch pays for itself!

FJC – Bring your own wine to dinner. Almost all restaurants have a corkage policy. This is a great bargain if your wine is expensive. One rule of etiquette – never bring a bottle that is on the restaurant's wine list.

*AFM* – I dine out since I am single. Generally it's almost a wash in terms of costs nowadays. Quality prepared meals are so good that cooking at home is becoming less logical. The waste and spoilage factor is high for a single guy buying basic groceries. Cooking is more of a hobby, habit, personal fulfillment exercise. Preparing meals is not really time efficient.

T&RR – We eat out for variety and when we feel like being frugal with our time. I hate to waste a good appetite on substandard food.

DES – Go to Happy Hour for your dinner…it will save you a lot.

AA – Try to limit eating dinner out to twice a week.

DLS – You can spend a lot of money eating out. Make sure you understand just how much it costs you.

*AFM* – Don't be a small tipper, you'll eventually get a reputation for being cheap. If you want to economize, eat in.

DTA – Look for great values when dining out vs. extravagant socializing places. You will feel better about it after your meal.

VNN – Only eat out for special occasions. Never eat fast food, it's a total waste of money.

*AFM* – You only live once – enjoy yourself within your means. You don't need to have a standing reservation at Tavern on the Green to enjoy friends, food and a nice glass of wine…or three.

### Entertainment

*AFM* – For home entertainment…try NetFlix or equivalent instead of expensive "on demand movies" on cable. Get TIVO so you can watch whatever you want whenever you want.

R&DW – After you have hit your expense and savings budget for the month feel free to spend the excess on whatever entertainment you enjoy.

B&GH – Entertainment coupon books sound good when you buy them, but never pay for themselves.

*AFM* – I spend a lot on "life experiences" rather than material things...thus heavy spending on travel and entertainment.

MW – I keep entertainment at a minimum but splurge on dinner and wine.

JMM&DRS – We love to entertain at home and have friends over for dinner far more than eating out. We have theater tickets, and go to a lot of movies, but also use NetFlix for those movies not worth seeing on the big screen.

## 8. Clothing

Fashion models get their clothes for free. Movie stars get their clothes for free. A lot of famous people get their clothes for free. Everyone who wants to look like them pays through the nose to do so. The frugal millionaires don't fall for this type of marketing.

Yes, we all have to "dress for the part" sometimes but we don't have to get on the fashion merry-go-round to do so. Frugal millionaires see clothing differently. They dress well with a traditional look, and they try to get that look at the lowest possible price without sacrificing quality. They do it by buying smart. They have some very simple but effective approaches that keep them (and their wallets) from being slaves to fashion.

## *Strategies*

JKB – Buy the best made clothes, not the cheapest. Get the help of a professional to build a simple wardrobe. You will buy less frequently and feel better about your self image.

*AFM* – Practice one simple rule: If I buy a new piece of clothing or shoes I have to get rid of at least one piece or pair of the same.

B&GH – Be comfortable. Impress with your mind, not your clothing. Never show up "shabby."

*AFM* – Buy the basics and keep the colors simple.

ERK – Use the 12 month rule: If you haven't worn it for 12 months throw it out. Make sure you pay attention to how much stuff you are throwing out.

*AFM* – Don't dress to impress other people. It's a sign of insecurity, and someone will always have better stuff.

*AFM* – Avoid being one of those people who is all "suits and shoes" and no "savings and security."

*AFM* – Don't get carried away on clothes. There's a point where you just can't wear everything or there is a price that just doesn't make sense. Be sensible. This is usually not a problem for men. Mostly it's the wives or girlfriends that get totally out of control. Nobody, but NOBODY, needs 100 pairs of shoes or 30 purses. They become trophies that women collect so they can show off to their girlfriends.

AD – Budget for your clothes and stick to it.

*AFM* – If you are constantly donating your clothes to charity then rethink what kind of clothes you are buying.

DLS – Wear clothes that make you feel good (while being appropriate for the situation), whether it is 20 year old shoes or a pair of beautiful gold cuff-links for a special occasion. But remember: Clothes do not make the man or woman.

VRN – Be as causal as you want and need to be. Shop Sam's and Target for the day-to-day stuff and Nordstrom for the weekend.

R&DW – Make sure that you wear what you are buying; the money you spent on your clothes is not making more money for you hanging in the closet unused.

VNN – You'd be surprised what you can get in a "vintage" or used clothing store. I actually spend very little on clothing and am considered very well dressed by most of my friends and colleagues.

*AFM* – Certain clothes might not be such a bargain if they always have to be dry-cleaned.

WCA – Stay fit, keep the same clothes for a long time and don't be a slave to fashion.

S&AW – Kids do fine with hand-me-downs.

BEH – Don't keep changing your wardrobe.

DES – Maintain the same size so that you don't have to keep buying clothes. Decide on your favorite colors so you can coordinate and have fewer clothes. Learn what discount places have the clothes you like.

DMG – I like to use a personal shopper to buy a few out-fits and get educated on the latest things. Then I use what I've learned to buy more outfits somewhere else.

### Designer wear

RDF – Personally, I believe high fashion is a waste of money.

AFM – Try to avoid logo clothing…you are not an adver-tising billboard.

VTN – I only *shop* the designer section of stores and then only *buy* off the sale rack.

AFM – Don't buy Armani if Nordstrom fits your needs and desires.

### Classics clothing

VNN – Pay well for classic items that you will wear for ten years or more.

KJH – I tend to buy clothes that have a timeless or classic look and that won't go out of style. I'm willing to spend a little more on good looking clothes, but won't spend a lot on the latest fashions.

AFM – Have a few really nice things (suits, pants, shirts and shoes). Buy the rest at Banana Republic or The GAP.

JLL – Keep it basic and classic. Buy quality, but buy it on sale.

AFM – Basic prep clothing has sustained me for my life.

### Timing

JMM&DRS – I like nice clothes, and I buy them on sale.

SR&BS – Buy nice clothes, but infrequently.

*AFM* – I only buy if it is on sale. I tend to buy staples mostly so these stay in style from year to year.

*AFM* – Buy clothes just once a season.

*AFM* – If you buy traditional clothes in the "off season" it won't matter because they won't go out of style. You just get a better deal.

### Style / quality

RJC – Buy clothes because you need them, not because they are a new style.

AA – Buy quality. It lasts longer and you feel better, even though the initial price is more expensive than the bargain rack.

*AFM* – If you buy expensive clothes that remain in style you can wear them longer due to quality materials and craftsmanship. In the long run this kind of expenditure is actually the better financial play.

ERK – You don't have to wear the latest and greatest, or what was fashionable in the 80's just to save money. Jeans and a black t-shirt look just fine in many situations.

*AFM* – Buy high quality stuff that rarely goes out of style.

*AFM* – High price doesn't always equal high quality.

### *Trendy*

*AFM* – Dress well for work, as required. The cost of clothing is a rip-off. Always buy quality clothing which will last rather than trendy clothing which will become expensive rags.

*AFM* – Don't waste your money on trendy crap. Most trendy stripes and patterns go out of style quickly anyway.

*AFM* – One or two trendy accessories (shoes!) can make the whole outfit up to date.

VNN – Buy accessories. Trendy accessories keep your look up to date. If trendy clothes are necessary then buy them cheap.

JT&B – If you want trendy – don't splurge – go buy it in the "teens" department.


## 9. Saving before spending

The economy runs on consumer spending. One trick to being a frugal millionaire is to *not* contribute more than your fair share to this segment of the economy. If you let others con-tribute instead you'll be in that small percentage of the pop-ulation that "gets it" and can potentially profit from it.

Frugal millionaires save before they spend, if they spend at all. Don't get me wrong, they will spend for good rea-son. But is has to be a really good reason.

You will have nothing to save if you spend it all first. That's the reason why saving comes before spending for the frugal millionaires. They have many proven ways to accomplish just that.

### *Saving strategies*

*AFM* – Save a lot before you spend a little. Invest it and let your money grow through compounding.

R&DW – Pre-determine a portion of income that will be saved and hold yourself accountable to at least that amount prior to spending anything.

*AFM* – Before you set up a savings account set up an "emergency fund"...with at least 6 months of living expenses. Then set up your savings account. (They should be separate accounts.) After that be careful not to do any frivolous spending.

DMG – Each time I got a raise I continued my current lifestyle and just saved more. Buying a ticket to financial freedom meant more to me than increasing my lifestyle with stuff.

JMM&DRS – We have a very strict annual savings goal that we adhere to.

*AFM* – Save as much as you can, and thoroughly enjoy what you buy.

JT&B – Thinking ahead helps. Use a budget if you need to.

DAS – Saving for tomorrow is important.

S&AW – Always work to save more than you spend. And start saving early, it is amazing what it can do for your sleeping habits.

*AFM* – Pay yourself first every payday.

*(This means, put money away in investments, savings
and retirement before you pay your bills. Always be
thinking about paying yourself before creating more bills
for yourself.)*

DTA – I can save because I live below my means.

BEH – I use all the financial vehicles available to save
money. I max out the company 401K and the Employee
Stock Purchase Plan (ESPP).

*AFM* – We have been very big savers and were both so
before we met. We either invested or saved about 50% of
our annual incomes each year. I invested because I never
wanted to be financially dependent on anyone...

JKB – Save 30% of what you make. Period.

### Spending strategies

*AFM* – View nearly every purchase as a "considered purchase" – meaning that you really need to think about
what you are spending your money on. It's more than OK
to have fun with your money, just don't over do it.

RDF – Spending money is not fun. If you need something,
buy it, but shopping for pleasure is the greatest way to
waste money *and* time.

*AFM* – Try to compute the costs of big things including what
they'd cost in "pre-tax" income. That's the income you have
to earn before you get your paycheck and then money in the
bank to spend. So, a $1,000 LCD TV might really cost over
$1,200-$1,400 in "pre-tax" money depending on your federal and state income tax bracket. And don't forget state and

local sales tax. That might make you really think twice about buying it because it's not just $1,000. Always think of it as 20%-40% more than "the price tag."

DES – I always ask myself "Is there a way I can get it for less?"...it's a game.

*AFM* – Tell your spouse/significant other what you each buy every day...otherwise you might get overdrawn at the bank. It helps you from being clueless about how all the miscellaneous spending adds up to big numbers.

RP – Don't just spend for the sake of spending.

*AFM* – Do your spending early in life. Then try to repeatedly recall the "joy of spending" that you got 20 years ago from some now useless VCR that you wasted money on vs. the $2,000 or $3,000 that money would be worth now if it was in a decent investment.

AA – Live by the golden rule – Don't let your spending exceed your income.

*AFM* – Pick some month to go really lean on your credit card. Rather than dreaming of saving money, do it by going hardcore frugal for just one month. See what happens.

*AFM* – As a general rule: If you can minimize the number of things you get a monthly bill for the better off financially you will be (cable, magazines, phone, cell phone and burglar alarm, etc.).

RJC – I always ask myself, does what I want to buy appreciate or depreciate in value? If it depreciates, think about it again, and ask yourself if you really need it or not.

ERK – Spending is much easier than saving. I have no clue why that is. Savings means you do nothing, spending takes effort. If your savings account or savings reserves are small in comparison to what your checking account looks like, you need to have a better plan.

### Combined strategies

JDS – There are three phases in a "well off" person's financial life. Accumulate, Preserve and Distribute. Figure out which one you are in and don't get tempted by the others.

MG&DG – Save monthly by directly deducting out of your checking account or paycheck. Spend less than you make.

JSB – Enjoy your money! I have found that one's attitude toward money as a whole is the most important thing a millionaire can have – as with most things in life, the greater the balance in life the greater the ease/happiness. The worst thing is to be scared to lose your money. Fear is a nasty worm that will invade all parts of your life if you allow it to take root in one of them, especially if it's your relationship to money. By the same token, recklessness with money is stupid (and for a New Englander, morally reprehensible).

AFM – Spend anything you want...PROVIDED that at the end of the month you have first put away savings and investment money according to your goals, and paid all your credit card debts.

B&GH – Budget yourself, even if you have lots of money. Decide what your annual "burn rate" can be and still meet your net goals.

VTN – When I was a child, my mother taught me to save half my earnings (babysitting money and the like). I still put aside money every month and have it withdrawn automatically. Whether you need to live on a budget or not, you still need to live on a budget. Then, when you want to splurge a little bit, it feels like a treat!

*AFM* – You can either piss your money away or put it away...your choice. If you do the former you'll be *really* pissed when you have nothing saved for your future.

T&RR – I'm frugal in the sense of not wanting to waste. One of the hardest things for me is to spend time on important purchases and not worry about those that are relatively small.

RME – First, I save 10% of my salary and invest it with my financial advisor. The rest goes to real estate investments. Second, I spend money to have fun.

*AFM* – My mindset is simple: I like to save, hate to spend.

*AFM* – Save and/or invest a large portion of your wages. Never pay full retail. Decide what you want/need and price shop.

*AFM* – The goal should be to have your net worth increase over time. Never let your net worth get below the minimum you need to sustain your family. You just want to make sure, that in general, more comes in than goes out. You should adjust your saving and spending accordingly.

*AFM* – Nobody ever got rich just by saving their way to it. You only get rich by generating income. You can offset the "getting rich" part by spending too much, but you can't get rich by saving alone.

AC – Be balanced by always saving and also spending for what you need. There are some times, opportunities and places that can't ever be recaptured. Live in the present AND plan for the future.

VRN – Save as much as you can, but enjoy life. Put $.50 in the bank for every $.50 you spend.

VNN – Develop an attitude that saving is better than spending.

*In Lehman's Terms:*
### THE MARKETING MACHINE

Why can't people hold on to their hard earned money? One of the frugal millionaires says:

*"Smart people spend their lives sitting in rooms figuring out how to convince you to spend money. You're smart too, if you need something go for it, but never buy anything on impulse."*

We are constantly told that we aren't cool if we don't have a certain credit card or wear a certain kind of designer sunglasses or jeans or drive a certain type of car or have big boobs and a skinny butt. Many marketers leverage the fact that we are all insecure about something. And what will make us momentarily strong or feel better is buying something...right now. How shallow is that? Very.

A sign for a shoe store in a high-end shopping mall once said, "Nothing cures the blues like a new pair of shoes." But it should have continued with: "And you'll be bluer yet when you see your monthly credit card debt!"

For the frugal millionaires, the only person influencing their spending decisions is them.

*In Lehman's Terms:*
## SPENDING ADVICE FROM HOROSCOPES?

Even the ever popular horoscopes have acknowledged America's inability to control their spending. As entertaining as they are...in some cases they are giving pretty decent spending advice.

Here are two of my favorite horoscopes:

"It's probably best to stay out of the stores if you can. You won't give a fig about how much you spend. You'll be easily seduced by flashy advertising. Leave your credit cards at home."
*– Linda Black*

"In order to keep up with your luxury-loving appetite, you must make more money. Develop habits that wealthy people have. Observe, read and find a mentor who will answer your questions."
*– Holiday Mathis*

## 10. Buying "stuff"

Buying "stuff" is a fact of life. But some people buy a bunch of "stuff" they just don't need. They think it will make them happy. Often it doesn't. Or maybe it's just the physical buying process that makes them happy? It probably doesn't. They get in debt. Their credit card bill comes in and they get unhappy very fast.

You'll see below that the frugal millionaires think about buying "stuff" well before they actually do it. And, they have some pretty creative ways in how they do it.

### Philosophies

*AFM* – Only buy something if you really need it. Think about it a lot before buying. Ask yourself what else you could be doing with the money first.

MG&DG – Prioritize and be content. Too many times we all want more stuff. That stuff does not bring happiness.

DMG – If in doubt, think about it overnight.

*AFM* – Be thoughtful about what you really want and balance the quality/price of that stuff with how important it is to you.

RP – Don't let "stuff" run your life.

DLS – Think about what you "want" versus what less fortunate people "need." Then make your buying decision.

*AFM* – If it makes you feel good and it doesn't impact your retirement plan then why not – this life is truly only one time.

AA – Only buy what you NEED.

AD – Consider needs vs. wants and the timing of what you are buying.

JSB – Don't agonize over buying small stuff, but when it comes to the big stuff – cars, boats, planes, houses – don't buy anything that you can't take care of yourself. The minute you have to hire a staff to take care of your "stuff," you have too much of it.

DES – Think it over before buying. Think through why you need it and will you really use it. Buy it used if possible. Make sure that what you buy has resale value in case you ever want to sell it.

DTA – Don't be impulsive. Think it through. Ask yourself: Do you really want it?

## Strategies

R&DW – Give yourself time to assure that you aren't making an "emotional purchase." If you still want it a month or two from now then you must really want it. Force yourself to do a "T" account of the positives and negatives of the purchase to help eliminate emotional buying. Then force yourself to answer the question: "Will I really use it?" or does it just sound nice? A lot of people get a high out of spending money and getting new things, but then don't really get what they imagined.

*AFM* – Rather than buying stuff just for you, think about buying stuff jointly with neighbors. Example: Consider going in with neighbors on a lawnmower or other yard equipment that everyone can use. Or share your lawnmower in trade for a neighbor's power tools. Most of the time these things just sit idle.

J&CB – We always try to buy used. We use the internet to find what we need. Fortunately we have come to a place in our lives where having a lot of stuff is rather meaningless.

JLL – Put yourself on a budget. Ask yourself how often you'll actually use something. Are you better off renting it?

VTN – In the past, when I've been feeling flush, I tended to buy a lot even though it was stuff I didn't really need. So now, I make myself wait for a day or two. If I'm still thinking about the item I can go back and get it. I rarely buy things when I'm traveling, because I can't return it if I change my mind. These days I rarely shop for anything. I don't need much at this point.

*AFM* – Use the "stuff" you want to buy as a "carrot" for being "good."

JMM&DRS – We do shop sales circulars and stock up on sales at grocery stores. We also buy in volume at Costco but they are not always the cheapest so we comparison shop some. Always go out after Christmas and buy cards, wrapping paper, etc., at 40-70% off for seasonal items.

VRN – Plan it out. Use cash. Never regret it. Make sure everything you buy will be used.

### Research

SLL – Look on the Internet. Research what you want to buy. Use price comparison engines. Consider the hassle of returns to an Internet seller compared to buying locally. Also compare local taxes vs. shipping costs. Know the market value of what you are buying. Ask how low the seller can go. Then offer less. If it's no deal then offer to buy a few more items at a great price to get a better deal and confuse the issue. I learned this trading monopoly properties as a kid.

MW – I buy what I want but I thoroughly research the products I buy to know what is going to have the best value over time and where to get the best price.

### To buy or not to buy

RJC – Pick something special periodically, but ask yourself: What is the long term value of it?

*AFM* – The stuff you buy depends on what kind of stuff it is. If it's not material like DVDs, buy all you want. You deserve it.

*AFM* – If you don't plan *ahead* when you are going to buy something you will be paying out the *behind* for it.

S&AW – Feel free to treat yourself every now and then, but do it because you accomplished something great like losing weight, etc.

*AFM* – If you are buying exotic cars or homes, be careful. One of the benefits when you have money is that you can be free to just buy the stuff you want. But, it needs to be reasonable. Don't show off or brag. People will think you are a jerk, and they'll be right.

B&GH – Buy the stuff that makes you happy. You only go around once. Keep all the packaging and manuals in case you need to return it or later want to sell it.

JKB – Never forget to take care of yourself. If you really want something then get it, as long as you can pay cash for it.

*AFM* – It is OK to indulge yourself in some manner, within reason.

JTA – Buy yourself a present when you close a big deal or get a promotion or something similar. Otherwise, ask yourself if it is a want or a need. How many similar things do you already have in a closet somewhere?

*AFM* – Reward yourself when you hit life milestones.

*AFM* – One word on buying stuff: DON'T. Ignoring the money component, I try to avoid buying because if the time and energy it takes. For every 1 trip I make to purchase, I make 1.4 trips to return it because it's broken or I am dissatisfied with it.

T&RR – Biggest problem is dealing with it once it's been bought.

S&AW – Don't buy large items on a whim.

### When to buy

RME – I purchase what I need, when I need it. I don't buy items because I'm getting a great deal.

RDF – Always wait. If you need it that's fine, but never buy anything in a store the first time you see it.

*AFM* – Splurge once a year.

*In Lehman's Terms:*
## SMART SPORTS GEAR BUYING

One frugal millionaire needed a new set of golf clubs, but realized that he only played 5 times per year. He decided he did not need anything more than a basic set of Wilson clubs for $115. (Other brands of clubs can sell for anywhere from a couple of hundred dollars to over a thousand dollars more.)

Talk about letting common sense take control over ego. Good job! He could have gone out and bought the best clubs on the market to try to impress everyone else. (Would your game really have improved?) But that would have been seen as a huge waste of money in this frugal millionaire's eyes. The clubs he bought were good, they fit the need, they were inexpensive, and economically he'll still be ahead when compared to renting clubs 5 times a year.

There are many lessons here...1) that we tend to over gear ourselves to excess (past our abilities) for something we might do only occasionally, and 2), it ends up costing a lot of money that doesn't need to be spent.

## 11. Buying personal electronics

People love buying electronic gadgets. Consumer electronics are big business and the marketing fueled feeding frenzy created around new product launches stimulates a tremendous amount of demand. But the frugal millionaires ask: Once the newness wears off what have you really got? Is it something that someone else had so you needed to match them and have it too? Did it make you cooler or smarter? Is it something that you will truly use once you've acquired it? The frugal millionaires know how tempting these products can be. So they create a strategy on how to deal with acquiring them.

### *Philosophies*

*AFM* – Don't buy an extended warranty for computers or electronics (or pretty much anything else) – unless you are really hard on your equipment. It's a waste of money and pure profit for the stores. They wouldn't sell this kind of "insurance" if they didn't make a lot of money on it.

SLL – Notebook computers are better than desktop computers for most people. They are quieter, smaller and more portable. They also use less energy.

RJC – Buy them only when needed. I bought a hot shot gaming computer…it broke all the time.

WAC – Don't try to keep up with the Joneses.

SR&BS – Too much junk complicates…keep it simple.

MG&DG – Gadgets take up money, time and energy. Limit the gadgets unless they truly save you substantial time. Invest in a BlackBerry or something similar.

RP – Buy functional.

## *Buying*

RME – I tend to buy the same computer because of the service and price. I do the same with cell phones. When it comes to audio/sound electronics I let my ears do the buying. For HDTV I let my eyes do the buying. Within reason of course.

*AFM* – Last years technology in a bundled package (computer, printer and/or digital camera) at an office supply store is usually the best all-around deal. They almost always have rebates. Check the websites of all the stores. Give away the stuff in the bundle that you don't want to charities or people who would need it.

JLL – Never buy at the beginning of a product lifecycle.

NM&JPR – Always buy for an intended use or specific requirements, and never because it's a fad.

*AFM* – Buy only as necessary, and do it online.

JT&B – When buying, ask if there are any corporate deals. Use mail-in rebates.

B&GH – Buy the best model you can afford. It will last longer before becoming obsolete. Check price comparison websites carefully before buying locally. Try to support locally owned businesses whenever it makes sense. If they give you good advice, reward them by buying there.

*AFM* – First question to ask yourself when buying a computer: What demands will I put on it? Then buy accordingly. For electronics: Are my audio/video tastes such that I need to buy a $4000 high end LCD TV from an equally high end store, or will the 52" one from Costco meet my needs?

*AFM* – Always wait for prices to drop.

*AFM* – Unless you can expense them or enjoy gadgets as a hobby, buy reliability and ease of use.

### New technology

DES – Don't buy cutting edge technology unless you need it for work. Last year's tech is always cheaper.

JSB – I always used to be the first one on the block with a new gizmo, but now I wait for the first revision and the drop in price. Being first was just an ego thing anyway.

*AFM* – I tend to take a "pass" on early electronics gear waiting for the bugs to get fixed and prices to come down after the manufacturer gets scale and finishes milking the early adopters for the highest prices. I'm lucky to get hand-me-downs from friends who "need" the latest gear and don't care if they get money for their old stuff.

JMM&DRS – We tend to be late adopters and replace items infrequently, usually when it breaks and not just when we find something cool to buy.

JLL – Wait until the "new one" comes out and buy the "old one" at a big discount!

VTN – I am a slow adopter and do not buy anything when it first comes out. So I just wait.

### Upgrades

RJC – I have a few Macs and old PCs. I simply upgraded them and they work well.

*AFM* – Just get a new computer before you ever consider going through the hassle of upgrading the operating system on your current machine…it's not worth the hours of pure frustration. Always have a back-up drive…and use it.

ERK – Keep your technology a bit longer than you would care to and you get a better replacement machine in the future, at a lower price. You don't need the latest, and you don't need the best.

*AFM* – If it works and is reliable, keep it for a while. Trading up to the next best new one will often create more headaches than benefits, although it's fun.

S&AW – We buy new phones and computers about once every three or more years.

## 12. Getting rid of "stuff" you don't need

People acquire stuff. Some of it is necessary for whatever stage of life they are in. Some of it is needed only temporarily and some of it will last a lifetime. Some of it is bought on impulse and once it resurfaces in a basement somewhere the question is often asked, "Why did I buy this?" Sound familiar?

Since people don't have unlimited storage they sometimes need to get rid of stuff. If the frugal millionaires need to get rid of stuff it's usually to simplify their lives or to give it to others who might need it more at the time. Here is how they do it.

## Philosophies

NM&JPR – We don't understand "don't need" – if it was a good purchase in the first place then it should continue to be needed.

AFM – Consider donating to a charity a portion of any money you make from selling your stuff and de-cluttering your world. It's a double reward.

RJC – If you don't use it, dump it.

R&DW – Either sell it or donate it for the write off, don't just throw it away out of ease.

AFM – Make it a major effort to not acquire stuff. Keeping life simple is a critical life philosophy.

## Strategies

AFM – Try giving it away first. What you can't give away to deserving people then donate it to a local charity in your community. If they don't want it, try to sell it on eBay or Craigslist or, post it for free or put it in front of your house with a "free" sign on it.

AFM – I purge every month. Having a home with little to no storage space makes you focus on what you really want and what you don't need.

*AFM* – I always clean out my stuff twice a year.

*AFM* – What we often don't realize is that we are annually heating and cooling a bunch of stuff we don't use or need. This costs money.

### Selling it

*AFM* – I'm big on this. Over the past year I have used Craigslist to sell all kinds of stuff. Netted about $1200 and put it in my son's college fund. It's found money!

DES – Once a year, around Christmas time, I go through the house/office and have my assistant sell anything that I don't need and I use the money for Christmas.

*AFM* – Plan to do a major purge by having an eBay broker deal with it.

B&GH – eBay and Craigslist are great places to sell. Check your buyers carefully. On Craigslist, only do local cash deals in person. Never agree to ship unless the buyer is a friend.

### Donating / giving it

SR&BS – Give it to friends, friend's kids, nanny, housekeeper, etc. Make other people happy with it.

*AFM* – It's not worth selling unless it's something big like a car or a second home. Better to give it away to the Salvation Army or a favorite school, church or charity.

DAS – It's usually easier (and better for others) to just give it away.

S&AW – We tend to give most of our items to Goodwill.

DTA – Donate it or throw it away. No garage sales!

AA – Give away things that you haven't used in two years – clothing, appliances and household goods.

*AFM* – We pack the family vehicle to the roof quarterly and head to the thrift shop. Our house has less clutter and we feel great about helping those in need.

RME – I donate stuff and take the tax deduction.

MJM – I give to Vietnam Vets on a regular basis. I also place things that I don't want by the garbage pick-up for those that can use my stuff – it's a form of recycling.

*AFM* – Don't sell it. Time is more important. Just give it to friend or family or donate it.

DC – Pass your stuff along to others who do need it. Selling stuff doesn't always have the same value as gifting.

## 13. Making donations / helping others

The frugal millionaires understand the concept of giving. They all do it.

The obvious thing that people might say here is that, "Of course they donate...they can afford it...I can't!" That sounds like an excuse that a cheapskate gives when they really don't want to support something. Donating isn't just something you only do when you have wealth. People always have something they can give to others. It's the best example of human nature.

Donations are often about more than money and can come in many forms. Frugal millionaires know that when you give (something, anything) to people you get a lot more back. You'll hear that sentiment echoed in the ideas below.

*REMINDER: 100% of the frugal millionaires said they donate money to charities or causes.*

### Philosophies

*AFM* – Give back, no matter what you have.

*JTA* – If you don't give back to your community by giving your time, your knowledge and your money to charity you are just plain selfish. I have probably made as much money or more than I have given to charity in the last 20 years from the relationships I have created from sitting on non-profit boards and being involved in charities.

*AFM* – Make a difference to the people in the community that you live in. You will feel great.

*WAL* – There's a saying "give and it will be given to you." If you have an attitude of poverty or being skimpy then you'll struggle to make money because you're too focused on it. The money you've created or your wealth is secondary to whatever you're doing in life. Ask these questions:

1) At work: Are you giving your all of the company?
2) At home: Are you sharing with responsibilities around the house with your spouse or significant other?

3) In social settings: Are you treating your friends to, or sharing with your friends or strangers, something they don't have but you do have?

It's difficult, but making this paradigm shift to an attitude of giving and sharing (yes, it seems counter-intuitive) has freed me from concern over money and focused me on doing or providing the best in my job, family and friends. This has opened doors for investments, found me new sources of income and has increased my regular 9-5 work income.

RDF – Don't make financial donations to charity if you don't have the money. Donate something else.

SR&BS – Don't ever feel pressured to give to organizations that your friends or family care about. It has to feel right to you.

JKB – Always give back some of what you make. It makes the world a better place.

S&AW – If you are given much in life – give back much. It is your duty as a citizen of this great country to invest in the things you love and pass it on so it is better than you found it.

VNN – It's important to give. It has been given to you so you need to give to others. I am a firm believer that money works in a "channel." If you open a channel for your money to flow out to others (that have less than you do) then money will flow back to you from the other end of the channel. Giving is a skill that must be learned and the more open you are to giving the more open you make yourself to receiving.

DLS – Make sure you understand how much of your donation is really getting to the people/programs that need it.

NM&JPR – Give carefully to small charities that make a difference.

JMM&DRS – We donate regularly and try to spend our values.

*AFM* – Pick a couple of causes you are passionate about and support them generously. Stay focused. It's easy to get drawn into a lot of causes and finding yourself in a touchy position of saying no to friends who ask.

MW – I make modest donations that are specific to things I truly care about.

JC – Look at the overhead of the charity for levels of efficiency, and then pick your causes carefully.

JSB – We only donate to operations that we are thoroughly familiar with, that have people we trust running them and know where our money is going. We pick mostly smaller charities or local organizations of bigger ones so we know we are actually making a difference.

*AFM* – This is essential for your mental health.

RME – The charity must mean something to me or my family and have administration costs that are minimal.

AA – Be generous, it's good for the soul.

MJM – I give to those who I am confident will put the money to good use.

*AFM* – The more you have the more your obligation is to give back and help others.

### Strategies

*AFM* – Make donations in the name of family members instead of buying holiday gifts that no one will remember the following year.

SR&BS – Give money away to organizations YOU care about. I once gave $3000 to a bunch of pre-school teachers with an anonymous note…they never knew it was me.

RP – Pick one or two charities that you can get involved with. Having wealth is a blessing if you treat it as such. Never flaunt it to anyone. Having money does not make you better than anyone. Be generous, but give for a good reason, not to impress anyone other than yourself. Spend your money and enjoy life, but without generosity you will feel empty.

*AFM* – Do a major donation, but set aside $100 for all the random ones that come along.

AD – Budget your donations annually.

B&GH – Don't make multi-year gifts. Give what makes sense this year and see where you are next year.

RJC – When you receive any wealth windfalls, chop away 10% immediately into a charitable trust. You never really owned that wealth and you'll thank yourself later for doing it.

*AFM* – Find local charities you like and regularly support them. Regular participation is more important than large amounts. A $50 check to your local food bank every year is more important that a $500 check to your college class reunion fund every 10 years.

### Time vs. money

*AFM* – Donate money *and/or* time...whichever you have the most of.

FJC – As you get older start making a donation strategy. Also, think about how you can give your time and skills.

*AFM* – I don't buy the arbitrary rule of donating 10% of your income to a church charity. It's an urban myth, like taking two months salary to buy an engagement ring. Guess who came up with those ideas? ...The people that benefit from them! On some days, I feel that my time is worth more than my money...so what kind of "credit" do I get for donating more of that from the "charity rule makers"?

DTA – Consider donating your professional services to people in need – especially in retirement.

VRN – Join a service club (Rotary, etc.) and stay focused on your philanthropy efforts.

### School donations

*AFM* – Donate regularly to your university. When it becomes more prominent it increases the value of your diploma.

SR&BS – When the guy raising money for the annual college fund calls for a gift, I said, "What are you giving? Tell me that, and tell me the truth...and I'll give that." He said nobody had ever asked him that before.

### Helping others

SR&BS – Loan/forgive loans to people who you care about.

FJC – Also use your money to support your family. It's great to include them in the will, but it is much better to give them the money now, when they really need it.

MG&DG – Helping others in need is the best thing you can do with your money. We take a portion of our money each month to help others.

*AFM* – Pay attention to tipping and recognize that what a few dollars might mean to you is much different than what it means to someone making minimum wage.

SR&BS – Teach your kids how to be generous. Have them give away toys they don't use. Have them conduct yard sales and send bags of stuff to orphanages.

T&RR – What about generosity towards family? One of the things I've learned is to ONLY give gifts that are specific and not recurring, such as a car, college education, etc. Never give a loan and never get into a situation where you are helping out to "tide someone over" during a rough spot. Those will never end and will change the nature of the relationship irreversibly.

### Tax deductions

*AFM* – I'd rather donate money than pay taxes. I'm still giving it away but I think I have better control over it.

ERK – I highly advise this. It comes off your taxes and helps spread wealth to those who don't have any.

T&RR – For donations we use highly appreciated stock whenever possible. It's very tax efficient. This is one of the benefits of being a limited partner in venture funds. Even if the fund does not do particularly well there is usually something that is highly appreciated to give away.

*A WORD ON DONATING HIGHLY APPRECIATED STOCK: It's a tax-savvy giving strategy that also allows you to receive – and give even more. Here's how it works: Instead of cashing out of a winning long term stock position and then writing a check to a charity, transfer ownership of the security – stocks, bonds, mutual funds and other assets – directly to the charity. This way, the charity books the investment at fair market value while you take an equivalent income tax deduction. Moreover, since the transaction avoids capital gains taxes, you can actually deduct more from your income than if you'd given straight cash. Keep that extra money, or give it away as well. It's a simple tactic, but surprisingly underused. More than two-thirds of respondents to a recent Fidelity Investments survey said they were unaware of the tax benefit of donating securities. (SOURCE: Marketwatch.com, with edits)*

AFM – Donations are a must do to share good fortune, but also for tax deductions.

BEH – Set up a charitable trust and have them do the homework on potential recipients.

## 14. Travel

Travel isn't the luxury that it used to be. We all know the reasons why. Even inexpensive travel is becoming more expensive. Being careful about what you spend when traveling has taken on a new importance, especially when we still want to enjoy our freedom to do so. The frugal millionaires are resourceful when it comes to getting what they want out of travel, but they do it for a fair value.

### Philosophies

*AFM* – Travel is the biggest consumer of cash for a family. Spend wisely.

JSB – I used to go for lowest rates and put up with the bad service, but no longer. It's worth it to deal with competent people who really care that they are doing a good job.

R&DW – With all the easy research that can be done on the Internet, great deals are available to be had with just a little time commitment.

*AFM* – Frequent flyer everything, you can do everything with points!

JLL – Sleep "cheap" and dine "fine."

*AFM* – I spend more money on travel since I favor experiential expenditures for life versus material acquisition.

NM&JPR – Don't go for the "top range" of anything…it is never worth the extra money.

### Strategies

*AFM* – Research the travel sites and then book direct with the airlines and hotels to avoid excess fees.

RJC – Fly coach! Use cheap rental cars and mid-level hotels. There are deals out there, find them.

VTN – I always vacation in the "shoulder" season so that I get the good weather of an area without paying the top prices.

JMM&DRS – We do our own travel arrangements, don't go on tours or have someone else put the package together.

VRN – Use the websites as much as you can, but learn that paying for the convenience of a travel agent is OK too if it saves you time and money.

S&AW – Use a single mileage credit card to build up points. We can't remember the last time we had to pay for a car rental because of certificates from American Express.

*AFM* – Put all your frequent flyer related numbers on one laminated card in your wallet so you don't have to carry a bunch of plastic. Keep one frequent flyer card with you to get through security faster if your airport offers a fast lane option. You'll save time, and that equals money.

B&GH – Listen to your friends and get first-hand referrals on places to visit and stay. Don't try to visit six countries in two weeks. You will feel exhausted. Try spending those two weeks in one or two places and really get to know the areas. Time spent packing and unpacking is wasted time.

*AFM* – Book in advance to get the best deals. Have frequent flyer, car rental and hotel memberships with everyone – it all adds up eventually.

ERK – Shop around, adjust days of travel if you are flexible.

*AFM* – Travel is very personal. Some people don't care about inconvenience at all. Others, including me, do. When I travel I want to be comfortable and have amenities. The extra costs are not that much in the long run, so it's worth it to me.

J&CB – Shop online. Use frequent flyer miles wisely (sometimes it's cheaper to just buy the regular tickets).

*AFM* – Cheap airfare doesn't always make for a cheap vacation. Check hotel and restaurant pricing at your intended destination before you book a "cheap" ticket. Know what you are in for before you get there.

RME – I tag on vacations to my funded speaking trips or business meetings to save money.

*AFM* – Decide how important travel is to you. I stay in top hotels and would not travel as much if I couldn't afford top notch accommodations.

MG&DG – Look for coupons online.

## *Air*

SR&BS – First class is not worth the dough.

JMM&DRS – We will shop for bargains and use frequent flyer miles for upgrades to business or first class. We would never pay for business or first.

JTA – Search out flights you want on Internet travel sites but then book directly on the airlines website. Otherwise, if you have a problem, the airlines will tell you to call whoever you booked through if it wasn't them.

BEH – No matter how much money you have you should still travel in coach.

*AFM* – I don't buy premium airfare. I would rather spend the money on other travel expenses.

DLS – If time is money (or precious) do what saves time, such as taking a more expensive direct flight instead of dealing with layovers.

## Hotels

*AFM* – Always try to get someone live on the phone at hotel reservations to see if you can get a better deal than online. Or at least to get a better cancellation policy than the online travel companies offer.

JMM&DRS – A hotel room is a place to sleep – it must be clean and safe but nothing else matters! We don't use suites and rarely brand name national or fancy brands. We love B&Bs.

DTA – I have a real problem paying over $200 a night for a hotel. I prefer to find unique places like bungalows and boutique hotels. Go with the local flavor, not the chains.

*AFM* – Always look for a deal on the web site of the hotel. If you don't see a deal, ask for one.

ERK – Don't always stay in the same hotel that you use for business during personal travel.

*AFM* – I will pay extra for a quality hotel since I spend more time there and it is the most key to the overall experience of travel.

*AFM* – Try "house-swapping" with people you know or legitimate home exchange agencies.

### *Rental cars*

*AFM* – Always get the smallest rental car you can. Chances are they might put you in a slightly better car because they will be out of the "loss leaders."

B&GH – Don't let rental car companies "upgrade" you to a van or an SUV. They are harder to drive, park and burn more gas.

SR&BS – Find a Town Car driver that you like, instead of taking a taxi, and let that be your decadence.

*AFM* – I rarely rent cars since it adds to stress and trip complexity.

ERK – There's nothing wrong with smaller cars when traveling on personal trips.

## 15. Health & exercise

Wealth is no fun without your health. With 66.3% of Americans being overweight or obese it is quite the challenge to find ways to stay healthy. *(SOURCE: Center for Disease Control, 2008)*. There aren't a lot of good role models around.

The frugal millionaires do everything they can to stay healthy. They know that being healthy doesn't have to be expensive, so they find simple and inexpensive ways to get their exercise.

*REMINDER: 100% of the frugal millionaires were NOT regular smokers. (Just three smoked an occasional cigar or cigarette.)*

### Philosophies

*AFM* – "Fat, drunk and stupid is no way to go through life, son." (From the movie *Animal House*)

*AFM* – Without health your money is worth very little, except that it might buy you a bit more (very expensive) time at the end of the road. Make good health a priority.

*AFM* – Investing in yourself is by far the best investment you can make – rest, exercise and proper fuel – this is NOT a cliché, this is an absolute fact.

ERK – Stay fit. Work out. It doesn't have to cost a ton.

S&AW – This is just like saving money: be disciplined. Feeling good, looking good and having a strong financial portfolio – it's all about a lifestyle commitment.

*AFM* – Plan for your physical health, not just your financial health. Health is important to me. I don't want to be that out of shape 300lb person on a scooter rolling around Disneyworld with my kids.

*AFM* – A healthy mind and body equals more freedom to enjoy your family and pursue success.

*AFM* – A moderate exercise regimen helps keep your sanity.

JKB – Do it. It's one of the best gifts you can give yourself and your family, in addition to reducing stress.

JLL – Make it part of your daily routine. Poor health will send you to the poor house.

*AFM* – Health is my number one priority. *Corpus sanum mens sana* (healthy body, healthy mind). As you become unhealthy you eventually burden your body, then your mind, and then all those around you.

B&GH – Get enough exercise so that you will still be around when your kids are grown. We have heard that grand-parenting is fun.

*AFM* – Try to balance length and quality of life with long term needs. Too many friends and family are stricken with illness or died early in life. I don't want to die without experiencing life as much as possible. Obviously this is tricky, so it's very intuitive as to when to spend and when to save, if in fact you do live a long and healthy life.

MW – I work out and try to eat healthy mostly for my own personal energy, but also because I want quality of life in my later years and don't want to have to pay for debilitating illnesses.

R&DW – You can't enjoy what you have worked so hard to build if you are not healthy – or dead.

### Strategies

JTA – You must stay in shape to stay on top of your game. Staying in shape sets a great example for your children as well. Exercise at least 3-4 times per week.

*AFM* – Keep an eye on your Body Mass Index (BMI) to make sure you are in a healthy range. Stop smoking.

DES – Take good care of your body by eating right and exercising. If you feel better you can work and play more. Also – cut your health insurance to "major catastrophe" and save money.

BEH – I am an avid runner. It is a necessity – I run several races every year including marathons.

JSB – Find something you enjoy for exercise and just do it.

SLL – Do yard work. There is always something to do. Avoid power tools, get a push mower. Try walking an average of a few miles each day. Pick a scenic route or do some errands.

MG&DG – Exercise regularly. Spend money on high quality, organic foods.

VNN – I believe in preventive maintenance. I spend lots of money each month on supplements that I know work for me. I have plenty of energy and rarely get sick. Find what works for you and use it.

AC – One of my "self-rules" is to always do something when I feel like doing nothing.

AA – You don't need to have money to exercise. Running is the best exercise and the cost of entry is a good pair of shoes and comfortable running clothes.

RME – My top priority after work every day is to get at least one hour of intense training in. I also walk my dog at least three times a week too.

*Gyms – yes*

JC – Clubs often run specials. Wait for one.

VTN – I joined an inexpensive gym near my house.

JT&B – We belong to the YMCA and take the kids there. We enjoy fitness.

J&CB – Never pay a monthly gym fee. Go to the gym and tell them you want to pay for an entire year at once. Then negotiate. You can save 20-40% off the membership that way.

### Gyms – no

*AFM* – Gyms are a waste of money.

RDF – A gym won't get you motivated. Get in shape. Go for a walk, go for a run, go for a swim, do push-ups or whatever.

*AFM* – The best gym is right out your front door. Bike, walk, hike…keep your body in motion. As the old saying goes, "If a shark doesn't stay in motion it will soon die."

*(NOTE: Sharks need water constantly running through their gills to breathe.)*

ERK – If you belong to a gym and never use it, cancel the membership and save the money. There's no reason to waste money just to not feel guilty.

*AFM* – Health clubs have great pricing and come-on marketing deals because they know that you won't keep showing up after a few months. Skip the clubs and just walk out your front door and get some inexpensive exercise.

### Personal trainers

*AFM* – You don't need to spend money on health because it can be very inexpensive. I will consult with a personal trainer, but not use one regularly for motivation. Set a lot of time aside for exercise. It is important.

JMM&DRS – Share a personal trainer with a friend for 2:1 pricing instead of 1:1.

VTN – I split my personal trainer meetings with a partner, so my cost is low.

NM&JPR – If you are too busy and the gym isn't working for you, get a personal trainer. They arrive at your door and force you into good exercise. It will be fun too!

### 16. Healthcare

Healthcare is expensive. I apologize for stating the obvious. Better technology to save more lives is necessary, but it doesn't necessarily make healthcare cheaper.

The best way to lower your medical costs is to stay healthy. Preventive care is very important to the frugal millionaires. If they are going to "overspend" anywhere it's going to be on healthcare, and they have found some interesting ways to do that.

### In general

*AFM* – The system is broken so stay as healthy as you can. You want "Mercedes quality" health care so don't be cheap. Be a smart consumer. Shop around and get second opinions. Don't spend more time shopping for a car than for your health care.

*AFM* – This is your responsibility. Find a great doctor and make sure he/she cares about you.

### Philosophies

MG&DG – Preventive care is essential to good health. Regular care is a priority.

RP – Go overboard on prevention.

T&RR – You still have to do your homework and seek out the best care. Simply having money does not mean that you will get the best care.

*AFM* – Make good health and dental care a habit, but not an obsession.

*AFM* – Maintenance is the best prevention. You get what you pay for.

WCA – Be an informed consumer, but let the medical professionals do their jobs.

### Strategies

*AFM* – Have a physical every year and get whatever tests your doctor recommends for your age group. Practice preventive health care…it's better for you and more cost effective.

BG&H – Find a doctor on retainer. That way he/she is on call for you 24x7.

*(NOTE: This is also called: a patient-supported medical practice or concierge medicine.)*

DES – Learn about alternative medicine and preventive medicine. You will feel better, spend less on medicine and doctors, and live longer.

*AFM* – Some people do more research when buying a TV than when they need a voluntary medical procedure done. The closest doctor to you or the most expensive one is not always the best choice. High price doesn't necessarily mean high quality. Sometimes it is the high overhead (office, staff, etc.) of a regional area or even a local neighborhood that causes prices to be high. Shop around. Get informed opinions. Make sure you know what you are paying for in every procedure and what follow-up is included. Quality of work can vary greatly from doctor to doctor.

### Health insurance

RJC – Be smart and get a catastrophic care plan. Start a small company or work for one so you can buy it cheaper.

JSB – This is brutal – I paid for a professional organization to do an assessment of where to best go for health insurance when I retired – They came back with the usual suspects (Blue Cross/Blue Shield) and I'm getting screwed with their rate increases and huge deductibles. You have no leverage if you aren't employed...which is a huge opportunity for someone to figure out.

*AFM* – Understand your company benefits and take full advantage of them.

DES – Save money by getting higher deductible medical insurance.

AA – Don't skimp. Purchase premium plans with maximum flexibility on choice of doctors.

FJC – Get the best medical insurance that you can find. This is one reason why I stay employed at a full time job.

### *Health savings accounts*

*DEFINITION: Health Savings Account – These plans allow you to save money to pay for future medical expenses on an income tax-free basis. Any individual, who has an approved High Deductible Health Plan (HDHP) and who is not covered under another disqualifying (= low deductible) health plan, can participate in an HSA. An employer can also offer Health Savings Accounts to employees and both the employer and employees are allowed to contribute funds to the HSA. (SOURCE: ehealthlink.com, with edits)*

*After the age of 65 HSA funds can be withdrawn for non-health related purposes, but you will have to pay income tax on the funds. (SOURCE: Smith Barney, with edits)*

RME – It's important to establish a Health Savings Account. Do not expect quality care with government intervention.

*AFM* – HSA plans are great even if you don't use every last dollar that you set aside.

## 17. Paying taxes

This is not everyone's favorite topic, but it's a fact of life in a civilized world. There are no magic bullets or secret schemes below on how to not pay taxes. They are an expense, like a lot of other things that can keep you from growing your net worth.

Frugal millionaires are willing to pay their fair share of taxes, but not more than that. And avoiding taxes doesn't mean evading them. Many of the legal "loop holes" have been eliminated over the years, so it's back to using the basic common sense principals of planning ahead, knowing what you'll be in for, and minimizing what you'll owe. The frugal millionaires have adopted an attitude towards taxes that makes them a lot less frustrating to deal with.

### *Philosophies*

FJC – Just pay the taxes. I got burned several times trying various tax shelters based on the advice of friends and financial advisors (including real estate shelters, oil and gas shelters and commodity straddles).

*AFM* – Avoid filing extensions and always pay your taxes on times. The penalties are a waste of money.

MG&DG – You've got to do it. Don't cheat the government. It will catch up with you.

T&RR – My wife and I had planned on moving out of our state because of taxes. However, we now have kids and feel like we're here at least until they grow up. Taxes never seem fair and we pay bunches.

S&AW – Take pride in being in an upper bracket, if you are. You should be honored if you are in the top 5%. Make wise choices in your investments so you limit your tax exposure.

*AFM* – Paying taxes is part of our responsibility for living in our society and being one of the lucky ones at a financial level. It saddens me to see people who have made a great deal of money going to great lengths to cheat the system and avoid paying taxes by doing things like pretending to live in a foreign country or the state of Nevada or using questionable tax tricks.

DTA – You have to do it. Don't sweat the stuff you can't control, but do minimize when you can. Don't lose sleep over your taxes.

*AFM* – The government is a bad investment, unfortunately it's a necessary one. Explore your options, take no risks and carefully pay as little as possible.

WCA – Pay what you owe. Don't cheat but don't pay a penny more than you owe. Purely tax motivated decisions are almost always poor ones.

*AFM* – Taxes are a requirement to support a democratic society, but that doesn't mean we need to roll over and support fiscal foolishness. Advocate those taxes in which you believe, fight those you don't, but pay them all as a good citizen. If you're unhappy on a net basis, Australia is a twelve hour flight away.

*AFM* – Pay what you owe. While it is always popular to complain about taxes we have a relatively good system compared to most countries.

NM&JPR – "Give unto Caesar…" And don't spend a fortune on accountant's bills.

## Strategies

JSB – Pay them if you have to…be careful setting up elaborate shelters as AMT gets applied very quickly now and disqualifies nearly every write-off.

*DEFINITION: Alternative Minimum Tax (AMT): An extra tax some people have to pay on top of the regular income tax. The original idea behind this tax was to prevent people with very high incomes from using special tax benefits to pay little or no tax. The AMT has increased its reach, however, and now applies to some people who don't have very high gross income (now $75,000) or who don't claim lots of special tax benefits. Proposals to repeal or reform the AMT have languished in Congress for years, but effective action does not appear to be on the horizon. Until Congress acts, almost anyone is a potential target for this tax.*

*The name comes from the way the tax works. The AMT provides an alternative set of rules for calculating your income tax. In theory these rules determine minimum amount of tax that someone with your income should be required to pay. If you're already paying at least that much because of the "regular" income tax, you don't have to pay AMT. But if your regular tax falls below this minimum, you have to make up the difference by paying alternative minimum tax. (SOURCE: Fairmark.com, with edits)*

ERK – Be smart about what you expense, be aggressive but stay within the lines.

*AFM* – Avoid quarterly taxes as much as you can, why should they make money on your money?

*AFM* – Overpay a little and get a refund. Avoid audits.

DES – Learn the tax laws so this can work to your advantage. It saves me the most money each year.

AA – Pay what you have to pay, but try to shift your income to lower capital gains rates.

J&CB – We do everything possible to reduce our tax burden.

### Minimizing taxes

VNN – Always itemize.

*AFM* – Pay what you have to, but maximize all your legal deductions. Start your year knowing how you can reduce your taxes and work towards that. The AMT is pure evil and outdated. Yeah, we should have a simple flat tax...blah, blah, blah...but until then just pay as little as you legally can and realize how fortunate you are. Bitching about taxes is so trite these days, be more intellectual than that.

AD – Minimize your taxes with charity donations.

*AFM* – Have your accountant analyze the merits of starting an LLC or creating a corporation. The tax saving implications can be immense. Creating an LLC or a Corporation is not that difficult, but check around on costs as they vary.

JDS – If you aren't making money you aren't paying taxes! Defer as much into legitimate tax advantaged vehicles as possible (401K, etc.).

## Accountants

RJC – Find a great accountant.

*AFM* – Get an astute accountant to do tax planning in advance.

ERK – Hire a professional as they will be able to talk to the IRS in the event any conversations need to be had.

*AFM* – Get a CPA. Do it right.

JKB – Tax laws are written to favor the government, not you. Seek the advice of a professional to minimize the impact and always consider additional taxes and save for them.

*AFM* – I don't spend large amounts of time and consideration here trying to save on taxes beyond my accountant's advice. Try to keep your life simple and just take the hit.

JC – Don't waste your time preparing your own tax return. Hire an expert to file for you. Be careful of AMT.

## 18. Conserving energy and water

As the price of energy (electricity, fuel and gas, etc.) continues to fluctuate we all find ourselves in the position of reminiscing about the good old days when energy was "cheap". The old days might seem to have provided "cheaper" sources of energy, but did we really think it was so cheap back then? Those of you who remember when gas hit a $1 a gallon didn't think that was cheap back then. Let's assume that those days may never come back (the likely case) and start to look forward with creativity and resourcefulness on conserving energy.

The UK and Europe have had to deal with high energy prices for years...and it hasn't killed them...yet. If you've always practiced conservation and have become highly efficient then even high energy prices will only require minimal adjustments to your lifestyle.

The frugal millionaires are keen on conserving and making the most of what they have. Here are their insights.

## *Philosophies*

*AFM* – I remember when I was a kid getting into the shower. The water was very cold. I went to turn on the hot water. My dad stopped me and said, "There are two ways of looking at everything. Rather than turning the hot water up higher, why don't you turn the cold water down?" That imagery has stuck with me to this day. I always look at a task with that thought in mind and ask how can I do something differently and prudently save money, while achieving the same goal?

ERK – Conserving is good for your wallet, great for the world and needs to be done.

KJH – Be frugal with more than just your money. Be prudent with our common resources and heritage for the sake of everyone now, and future generations.

*AFM* – It's not about money, it's about leaving the world a better place.

AD – Instill the practice of conservation in your children.

*AFM* – Everything that's in your control should be as efficient as possible. If you are going to spend money on something make it something that saves resources.

*AFM* – Don't waste. It's just not smart and it's arrogant and greedy. Use what you need but don't waste. Train your kids to do the same.

MJM – To not conserve is to be selfish.

**Go green!**

DMG – Walk to get groceries or run errands when possible. Make a big circle and don't backtrack when you run errands in your car.

*AFM* – If your lawn is small enough, and it's time for a new mower, get a push or electric/battery version. The gas powered models pollute wildly and they are too noisy.

*AFM* – Low MPG SUVs aren't fashionable or impressive (and probably never were!), especially if you are the ONLY one driving in it. Those who own them now understand this...ouch! Buy a small and efficient used car to get you from point A to point B. Don't be a slave to your vehicle...it's NOT a fashion accessory.

ERK – Change to fluorescent bulbs, turn off faucets, shut off lights and don't leave appliances or "ready-state" energy devices plugged in if you aren't using them.

JKB – Walk or ride a bike when you can.

RME – I take fast showers and wash my car after it rains.

*AFM* – Bike or walk for exercise when running errands rather than driving your car to the gym or store.

MW – We have an incentive program to ensure our kids conserve water and energy.

S&AW – We keep the house at 60-65 degrees in the winter. Wear a sweater and put an extra blanket on your bed, you'll sleep better.

*AFM* – LCD TVs are more efficient than Plasma.

J&CB – We even turned off our home phones and only use cell. That saved us $50 a month.

JLL – Always turn out the lights when you leave the room (unless your spouse is still in it!).

J&CB – We turn off lights, AC and Heat. We keep graphs of usage. Conserving is something within control of everyone.

*AFM* – Unplug your appliances, it will save energy and money. It's amazing how few of us know this. I am very close to getting "off the grid."

RME – I turn down the AC when I leave the house and turn it back up when I arrive home. Do the same with the office.

JKB – Buy a new front-load washer/dryer. Keep the thermostat set low on your water heater.

*AFM* – Unplug your hot tub. Better yet, get rid of it.

*AFM* – Use fluorescent bulbs in your house. Get a re-circulating hot water system that keeps pipes ready to deliver hot water. None of this costs much, but it has a quick impact on saving money.

RJC – Landscape with low water plants. Have your thermostat change to lower/higher (more efficient) temperatures when you are not around or already sleeping.

*AFM* – I replaced 80% of the bulbs in my house with fluorescent and my electric bill went down by $45 a month.

DES – Get the smallest garbage can possible so you don't get hit with extra utility fees.

JT&B – Use water timers! And, turn the heat/cooling down during the day.

## *In Lehman's Terms:*
## WASTING VALUABLE RESOURCES

If you are wealthy it means you can pretty much buy anything you want. But does that entitle you to waste more than others? No. One of the reasons the frugal millionaires became wealthy in the first place was that they are careful with their financial resources. They are also careful with all their other resources, like water, fuel, gas and electricity, etc. If you waste anything then you are ultimately wasting money.

Many people feel that they have the right to waste fuel...like driving gas sucking vehicles (size doesn't matter) and wasting other natural resources...if they can afford to. You see it every day. It wasn't until gas prices increased dramatically that many people started to understand that wasting anything isn't a good idea. Sometimes that's what it takes to change a bad habit.

Just because someone has the money to spend on these valuable resources doesn't mean they get to go to the head of the line when it comes to wasting them. The frugal millionaires know that wasting is never a good idea. We all need to practice being frugal with things that we will run out of first. Think of it as a long term gift to your kids and their kids.

## 19. Recycling / re-using

In addition to the concept of conserving resources, you can get full value from the things you already have by recycling and reusing them. Not only does that mean buying smart in the first place, it also means making things last as long as possible and even repurposing them once their initial useful life has passed.

The frugal millionaires constantly think about recycling and reusing. Most of them share a common philosophy on this and have many thoughts about how to recycle and re-use. They have plenty of practice at getting the most out of their money, so getting the most out of everything else comes naturally to them.

### *Philosophies*

*AFM* – Do the best to not waste anything. Sure, some country somewhere can always make more stuff for us...but where are we going to put all the old stuff? It's got to end up somewhere! It all starts with everyone's buying habits. If you stop buying junk products that don't last companies will stop making them. Buy with an eye towards getting maximum usage over a long period of time. We are all responsible for the future...don't think someone *else* will be responsible for that! Set a good example.

*AFM* – Recycle. Just do it. Leave the world a healthier place for your kids and their kids.

*AFM* – Recycle aggressively...it's good for the environment and it teaches self discipline.

DLS – No matter how much money you have you can still recycle.

*AFM* – Leave as little a footprint on Mother Nature as possible.

*AFM* – It's a social responsibility, it helps, and it's not that hard.

JKB – We are a disposable society. Buy high quality items that last longer and care for them properly.

*AFM* – Recycling is about treating the planet with respect and managing it for our children's children.

MJM – Recycle in earnest.

### Green strategies

J&CB – We try to get as much out of everything as possible. We throw nothing away until there is nothing else that can be done with it. We own many rental properties so we drive through wealthier neighborhoods and pick up appliances that have been put on the curb. We recycle their stuff for them!

ERK – Figure out a simple system that allows you to recycle without too much effort.

MG&DG – Recycle whenever and wherever possible. Don't use bottled water, instead purchase a filtration system in your home.

VTN – I have a weird habit of washing out plastic ziplock bags. It drives me crazy to throw those away.

JMM&DRS – We use the daily newspaper plastic bag to scoop dog poop, it works really well!

JT&B – We bring old bags to the stores to get groceries and to use for the kids sandwiches.

DES – Be organized so you can save valuable things that you can reuse, but you have to be able to find them.

JMM&DRS – We definitely recycle and reuse and also re-gift. We're not afraid to give our friends stuff we don't use or don't want anymore. We tend to share tips on these things with our friends.

*AFM* – Think about all the people who are drinking water from a disposable water bottle every day. Then think about those millions of bottles in your back yard. They are actually being dumped in everyone's back yard every day.

## 20. Attending "free" money making seminars

We've all seen the direct mail, infomercials and ads on television or in the newspapers and magazines that promise some seminar will set you free financially. Perhaps we bought a personal finance book and found it full of invitations to "free" seminars on how to get rich in some way or another. Did the frugal millionaires create their wealth by attending these "free" seminars? The resounding answer is: NO!

Even some of the purveyors of these free seminars know that they have a marketing problem and are starting to convert their "free" seminars to "fee" seminars. Their target market will soon figure out that nothing has changed…except that they are now paying for the same information.

When it comes to making money sometimes it is what you choose not to do that can help you grow your wealth.

If you choose not to attend any of those free seminars then you will have a clearer mind and time to do more important things...like focusing on what is really important financially.

You're about to get an earful from the frugal millionaires on this topic. They are pretty passionate in their opinions. Listening to them will save you a lot of time, money and frustration.

*REMINDER: Seven of the frugal millionaires (10%) had attended a "free" money making seminar with topics like: how to make money in real estate, or, how to think like a millionaire, etc. Only one out of the 70 frugal millionaires said they got something out of these seminars and would go back.*

That should say it all, but in case you need more:

### *Why they won't consider attending them*

*AFM* – This is marketing in its ugliest disguise.

VNN – Nothing is really free. Making money, like losing weight, is mostly common sense and discipline. You aren't going to learn those things in a seminar.

JKB – Hell no, I have not been to any of these. They are a ploy to make money off the ignorance and hope of others.

*AFM* – You must be kidding...they are scams.

JDS – They rarely make millionaires out of anyone except the charlatan.

JSB – These are a waste of time...much better to attach yourself to someone already in the flow who has made all the mistakes you no doubt would make on your own. I have never made money in anything right off the bat – it's like poker – you are the patsy until you gain enough experience to know how to win.

*AFM* – I'm all for staying educated on financial opportunities and strategies...but these seminars are clearly *not* the way to do it.

J&CB – I'm fascinated with, and at the same time appalled, at the efficiency with which these schemes separate people from their money.

AA – They are bogus sham attempts to fleece vulnerable people.

*AFM* – I don't think that those who have the ability to earn a million are in the target audience. It's just a media franchise extension for authors and publishers.

MW – Lot's of hype with little substance. In short, the only one making the money is the seminar organizer

*AFM* – Nothing is free. They are trying to sell something. It's a waste of time to be sold for a cheap lunch or dinner.

DC – It all comes down to execution. No amount of planning or dreaming will get you to your dream. And those who are teaching have figured out how to make money from others.

JC – They are generally BS. It's an opportunity for over-priced, questionable service providers to pitch generally unsophisticated attendees.

RP – They are a good way to become rich if you are the one giving them. They all tout that the millionaires giving the free presentations do so because they want to share – give me a break! They may be free to attend, but they have something to sell.

JMM&DRS – They are marketing programs for some "system"...not for us!

*AFM* – I have never felt that the systems that were successful for the "author" were a strong solution that was replicable for others.

*AFM* – I'm not a big fan. They seem like kind of a sham preying on people who fall victim to these "get rich quick" types of things.

DLS – I guess not having gone to any says a lot.

SLL – These guys are usually hucksters just trying to take your money.

R&DW – My opinion is that very little can be learned and obvious information is being shared. Or it's a money manager trying to find potential clients, or a get rich scheme trying to sell methods.

### *Mixed opinions*

*AFM* – Whether they are good depends on who gives them. If they are given by major guys like Trump then they are probably worth going to. However, a big part of the success formula in these things is personal intelligence and charisma of the presenter, mostly the latter. There are basic principles in these seminars that are consistent and valid. Hearing them from a proven success can be a motivator. It is always worth getting advice from proven successful people, but what they say is not a magic formula. You have to take the nuggets that they give you and apply them to your own abilities and situation.

VRN – Good educational value – but I get more from colleagues and industry professionals.

WCA – If such a meeting offered specific plans or approaches other than "woo-woo" psycho-babble about getting your mind into the right place, then maybe it would be worthwhile.

WAL – I have talked to several people that have been to these, from my conclusion it's all about what you put into it, there's a saying in data base programming "GI-GO" garbage in, garbage out. Don't waste your time if you approach the seminar with an attitude of suspicion. Don't go if you have that attitude – you're wasting everybody's time. One friend tried the "timing the stock market by day trading" program and had limited success and is now out of it; another tried the "purchasing distressed real estate" program and kept with it for a while and is also now out of it, but with his continued re-investment he is now a developer with commercial properties. Seminars are OK as long as you're not hooked into their product for you're success.

VTN – They are cheesy in delivery, but often accurate in their content. So much of what you make of yourself is in your own spirit, which is what I hear those seminars espousing. If you are passionate enough you could make money selling garbage, which is what these seminars are often about.

DMG – I attended a number of free seminars. I find them interesting, but have never purchased what they were selling. They usually have a "too good to be true" smell to them.

AD – They give you real basic knowledge after that it becomes a long sales pitch for some product.

JTA – I have attended free seminars and may again some day. I feel people can always learn from other's ideas and sales techniques and they don't have to learn from the bottom up. I don't feel that someone should buy all the tapes, etc. that are sold from the people putting on the seminars.

### Yes, I like them

DES – I took courses from one company and they were far from "free"...about $5K a week or for a few days. The return was well worth it and I plan on taking more.

*In Lehman's Terms:*
## NOTHING IN LIFE IS FREE...
## LIKE A "FREE" SEMINAR

You haven't lived a completely full life until you've seen the dark side of marketing in action. Yes, I'm talking about those "free" money making seminars that promise you financial freedom.

R-i-ight.

Let's be clear up front: These seminars are far from free. At a minimum they cost your time (which for most of us is worth more than money). They also cost fuel, parking and food, and, possibly, airfare, lodging, rental car, credit counseling fees and a psychotherapist bill.

These types of marketing vehicles aren't 100% bad if you can separate out the bits of good info from the gratuitous sales pitches. But there's only about 15% of the "good stuff" intertwined with the subtle (and often hard) selling. Sometimes you can see the difference, other times you can't. It's hard to tell if what they are "teaching" you for free is just a set-up to sell you something later. You also have to be able to remember the little jewels of wisdom they impart and put them to use if you expect to truly see a benefit. That is often easier said than done.

These presentations are polished to a smooth, super high-gloss finish, and delivered in a folksy, personalized kind of way. That allows the slime to slide right off them and down on to you. If you go to one of these seminars wear your foul weather gear because you are going to get slimed. I subjected myself to one of these free seminars "for the sake of research." I took a bullet for you.

Here is my story:

The seminar I attended started with two announcements for...you guessed it: an upgrade offer from the "free" seats to paid ones right up front. At least they were smiling about it. It didn't get any better from there. From that point on the presentations were fast, furious, deliberate, and designed to catch you in a weak emotional moment and sell you something. And typically right before a meal. Manipulative? You bet!

The motivational presenters (or should I say: carnival hawkers?) ask your permission to pitch you by making the content being delivered appear to be something extremely valuable and life changing. And because they've been bending your brain, heart and emotions for hours (sometimes days) you react to their "no-option but yes" request to tell you more about their paid programs. I watched people cheer them on like lemmings. Pricey self-improvement and financial growth programs get heavily "discounted" just for this seminar with the added pressure that "there will be only a limited number of seats available for these programs, at this special price." And since these programs will bring you love and happiness, make you rich and set you free financially how could you NOT be jumping up and down for this heck of a deal, they ask? What is wrong with you? That's the implied and sometimes obvious message anyway. The pressure continues...don't you know that by saying no you will be missing a huge opportunity that is being offered because we love you and want you to help us change the world? (Insert the "We are the World" hand holding sing-along here.)

As the pitching escalates, the room starts buzzing and the announcement is made that whatever they are pushing (um, offering) is "first come – first serve." Don't miss out! Only limited seating at these programs is available – right now! Now, Now, Now! The feeding frenzy tilts to a fever pitch. Buy now! You can hear the suckers in the audience agreeing under their breath by mumbling, "Uh-huh...That's right! Yes, that's right! Yes, Yes, Uh-Hum!" The fire and brimstone yelling and screaming is working...and you are now hooked...or at least considering it! I witness people jumping out of their seats and heading to the back of the room before the meal break to capture the deals before they are sold out and gone forever! Forever!

You can almost see dollar signs in the hopeful eyes of these people...like they have just found the key to financial nirvana...and it was oh so easy. It was like they were the only ones on the planet who were going to have access to this miracle financial cure. All they had to do was just show up today and all their financial problems (among others) would be solved. As long as they bought the seminar package! Quick, quick, run to the back of the room before you blow the opportunity of a lifetime! Get moving. Have your credit card ready please! And if you can't afford it right now we will let you make payments! Yikes!

I am not making this up!

You are told that to be successful you will have to fight your brain's default mode of trying to protect you and break out of your comfort zone (while your bank account gets broken into…) to commit to this life changing opportunity. Blah, Blah, Blah…

"Not so fast!," the conscience of many of the frugal millionaires would say! They didn't get where they are by falling for this kind of stuff. Why so? They are a financially savvy group, and hardly the target audience for these slicksters. That's why they don't go to these "free" seminars. All this "we're helping you to be a better person" stuff is being offered by the promoters with no substantive proof that these programs help the *majority* of the people who ultimately pay to attend them…even though some obviously positive testimonials are offered (of course!). A handful of success stories become the poster child for everyone's dreams and hopes. It's an all emotional "you can be smart like us" pitch which, as the frugal millionaires know all too well, is a sign to hold on to your wallet…with both hands.

The pitch continues to be made for the paid programs right before the lunch break is announced. The motivational presenter is winding down the pressurized pitch as the quotas in the back of the room are being filled. He is notably ignoring the people in the audience who are raising their hands right in front of him to ask questions. He continues to ignore them. Don't these attendees know this is a one-way presentation with only controlled interaction? No hard questions please! Just hand over your money.

What I saw was astounding. But you can't be a naysayer in this crowd or you will be labeled as someone who doesn't want to change their life for the better. Well, there are plenty of ways to change your life for the better, and for all but one of the frugal millionaires who attended these events this isn't one of them.

I'd personally like to thank all the people who collectively spent hundreds of thousands of dollars (!) during the seminar I attended so it could be offered to me for "free," relatively speaking anyway. But next time can the organizers at least comp the parking if they are going to relentlessly try to sell me their paid programs for hours and days on end?

## 21. Marriage

Marriage is viewed by many as a great institution. Unfortunately, half of the time that institution ends in divorce. But we remain optimists and we try, try again. The frugal millionaires have a lot to say about the financial side of marriage. They have a practical and common sense view that more people should consider before they take the proverbial "plunge."

*NOTE: All of the frugal millionaires in this section are listed as an AFM (Anonymous Frugal Millionaire). I'm just doing my small part to help those who are married stay married!*

*REMINDER: 83% of the frugal millionaires are married.*

### Marry for love or money...or both?

*AFM* – Marry for love first, and then for a similar approach to money. And marry someone who looks at money the same way you do or you won't have either love or money in the long run.

*AFM* – Marry someone who works harder than you, is smarter than you, makes more money than you and is better looking than you, and you will be just fine.

*AFM* – If they already have money that's a big plus! Money differences are one of the biggest reasons for divorce.

*AFM* – There are tens of millions of people in this world, of which there are millions of beautiful ones. Of those, there are hundreds of thousands who you would find attractive and of them there are tens of thousands who will equally find you attractive. Of those there are thousands who are very wealthy – so make your best effort to *fall in love* with one of the wealthy ones as it is just as easy to love a wealthy one as it is to fall in love with one of the millions of poor flakes in this world.

*AFM* – Be extremely careful about who you marry.

### Pre-nuptial agreements

*REMINDER: 60% of the frugal millionaires said they thought a pre-nuptial agreement was a good idea.*

*AFM* – While pre-nups are generally used if there is a big disparity in income they would also be an excellent idea even if partners are at relative parity in their financial situations.

*AFM* – If you don't have them (a pre-nup) you run the risk of losing half of everything.

*AFM* – Be fair with a pre-nup. It is important to know exactly what will happen if things don't work out the way you think they will.

*AFM* – Would you make an unprotected investment in *anything* if you knew for sure that it had a 50% chance of failing?

*AFM* – Protect your assets that you take into the marriage and the growth of those assets during the marriage, and until it ends. Hopefully it won't ever end, until one of you passes on. Start the pre-nup process at least six months before you intend to get married. Have it signed three months before you get married. Make sure that your fiancé has equal or better legal representation than you do.

*AFM* – Pre-nups are a good idea if one spouse has significant separate property.

*AFM* – If you get married quickly you can also lose your asset base just as quickly if it ever ends. Don't marry spontaneously if you have a lot of money to protect (or any money at all!).

*AFM* – Work with an attorney to make sure that you have the intent and goal of the pre-nuptial agreement in place before you get to the details.

*AFM* – Know all about your potential spouse's finances and assets before you write up a pre-nup and get married.

*AFM* – Should you get married or remarried later in life make sure that a pre-nup (and your wills and trusts) reflects your desire to protect your spouse and your family assets.

### Thinking alike about money

*AFM* – A divorce lawyer once told me that the finance person where your significant other bought their last car knows more about your significant other's finances than you probably do! Know as much as you can about how someone saves and spends their money before you get married…and what they might do with yours.

*AFM* – Spenders don't work well with scrimpers and savers. If someone can't show financial restraint in spending that is a deal breaker. Women have a responsibility to NOT need to be taken care of. Stay at home wives/moms who only go shopping and to the gym can lose their sense of self worth – and a man can't be everything to them. I will tell my children this: Find happiness, find someone that is equal in education, career and on the same page about money.

*AFM* – Marrying someone with the same values about money that you have is one real key to a happy marriage. Otherwise, fighting about money can never really be resolved.

### Common goals

*AFM* – Strangely, marriage as it relates to money is the hardest when the goals are seemingly 100% similar; that is, the two people have some level of frugality, so there's no argument there, and also similar goals on saving money. But then neither thinks their approach to spending money is the wasteful one. It would almost be better if one was a miser and the other spent like crazy...which might lead to a quick divorce, oh well. The hard part is trust; that is: my spouse trusts me to make the big life changing financial decisions, and arguably I've done well, but like all people I've made some big mistakes. Then I trust her to make the daily decisions and for her to spot all her wasteful ways. Arguably her pissing away a few hundred dollars too much on clothing is nothing compared to some of the bonehead financial moves I've made. But that's super hard to keep in perspective when it's spending vs. investing.

*AFM* – As a couple we talk about everything – there is no "given" in our relationship such as the person who makes more money or is worth more money, should pay more or that our opportunities are different. You should challenge yourself to think about the roles played by people in a relationship as it relates to money. How do couples with a stay at home dad, or lesbian or gay couples deal with the role of the "bread winner"?

*AFM* – The first rule of money and marriage is: Don't marry someone who is financially stupid (aka: bad with money). A lifetime of pain will ensue. The approach we have is to have ground rules about how money is spent and what the priorities are. We come to an agreement on what things are important to us both individually and to the family. Here are some things that are important to both of us that cost money and are worth spending it on: the house and yard, family vacations, private schools and the community tennis club. Here are things that would be fun, but we've agreed to not spend money on: wine clubs, expensive tennis clubs, expensive furniture, new cars every 5 years and saving up for "more of a house." The bottom line is although it may be cool to be quite different with your spouse in many ways...it tends to be good if you are quite similar as far as money goes.

*AFM* – It is critical to have your spouse completely aligned with your family financial strategy. Partners can have very different expectations about when and where to be "frugal." What constitutes a "luxury" for one might be considered a "necessity" for the other. A very frank conversation should be had early on to establish agreement on common baseline spending and savings plans. (This might rank up there in importance with the "how many kids" and "how will we raise them" conversation!) Beyond that, each spouse should have control over their own discretionary "budgets." I wouldn't ever call this an "allowance"! A prenuptial might come in very handy if you do call it that!

### Budgets

*AFM* – Always agree on the fixed budget for the hard dollar costs of managing the household. If you do not have a budget, make one. If it fluctuates measure it over a four-month period, take the high and use that. We have mutually agreed that if we are going to spend over $100 on any one item that falls outside the household budget, we will contact the other before buying. Key Point: Always remember the money you bring in does not belong to you, it belongs to your family. That's why they call it "bringing home the bacon" you're not going to feel bad if your family eats the bacon so don't feel bad when they use the money as long as they use it wisely. If you need the satisfaction of your "mad money" add an amount to your monthly budget, then cut it half and share it with your spouse. Money resentment will kill your marriage as it builds over time. If you have a problem with the way your spouse spends money just stop, take a deep breath and write down what the problems are. Organize and clarify them in a way you can understand. This process will help you when you approach your partner to discuss the matter and it will help relieve some of the low level anxiety you feel about your partner's actions.

*AFM* – It usually makes sense to "divide and conquer" when it comes to household finances and recordkeeping. You don't ever want to have two people trying to balance the same checkbook! Designate one person to manage and pay the common bills. Gain agreement on whose paychecks go where, how much goes into various retirement and investment accounts. Keep separate credit cards. Work together to create and understand your investment strategy. On decisions involving a significant portion of assets, make sure that both parties agree and understand the risks of the decision. You never want to have to listen to: "I told you so!"

## *Longevity*

*AFM* – We've been married for 30 years! Having one spouse is a real key to net worth. (Most of our friends who view themselves as "poor" lost half their net worth in a divorce!)

*AFM* – Choose wisely and stick to your marriage, it will be the best investment that you make. And when the market (relationship) gets choppy, don't bail...work hard and see it through.

*AFM* – Marry for keeps. Stay in it for the long haul...unless getting out is your last resort or there are abuse issues.

## *Family*

*AFM* – The most expensive thing in life is a wife and kids. If you pick wrong, assume that when you get married your wife will drive your level of spending and indulgence to levels you never would have imagined on your own. Kids cost a fortune for the essentials but also for all the training, activities, trips and education, etc. If you are going to have them then you owe them a certain level of investment.

*AFM* – Spouses can take on a life of their own and cost you a fortune. Make sure you either have unlimited pockets or, that from day one, you lay down the mutual rules and stick to them. Once it gets out of hand there is no way of reeling it all back in without serious measures that you don't want to take.

## 22. Paying for education

The more educated someone is the better their chances for success are in the real world. Education can come in many forms and it costs money. But, spending a lot for it doesn't guarantee success. The frugal millionaires place an importance on education, especially for their children, and have many approaches on how to fund these endeavors and make them work for everyone involved.

### *Philosophies*

*AFM* – Start saving for college when your kids are born. Leverage compounding.

NM&JPR – Put aside the money for your kid's education so that it will see them through their school years regardless of your changing circumstances.

JDS – After your house and basic retirement needs, is there a higher priority than your children's education?

DTA – Don't compromise your retirement to send your kid(s) to school, but it is part of your personal obligation. We talk about public vs. private education and who will pay for undergrad vs. advanced degrees. Public schools in most states are more representative of the real world. The people skills they will learn in college are more important than just being book smart.

JLL – Paying for your children's education is your best investment.

J&CB – Paying for your kid's education is mandatory.

JTA – Start putting money away early for your children, and teach them to be FRUGAL.

*AFM* – Consider the value of private vs. public pre-college education. A public education will get you into college and a private education will let you excel at college. It's an expensive choice...or is it?

*AFM* – State schools are best – your kids will get a better sense of the real world.

JMM&RDS – Public schools were good enough for us, why spend all that extra money?

### *"Who pays?" strategies*

*AFM* – Pay for all of your kid's education and have them pay you half of it back after they graduate and get a job. This is what my parents did with me, that way I had a vested interest in my education as well...and it made me work harder and get more out of college and graduate school. I'm not sure whether going to a state or private university makes as much difference for your kid's as what they choose to do when they are there. Having that conversation in advance about learning a profession that can actually pay for the education they are getting could make the whole proposition less costly.

*AFM* – Pay for as much of your children's education as possible, without diverting too much money away from your retirement and ending up as a financial burden on them.

MW – My parent's paid tuition, less the scholarships, and if I lost the scholarships I had to pay the difference. I paid room, board, books and all spending money...and thus averaged about a 30 hour work week during school and had my own business in the summers working 7 days a week. However, I am paying for my children's education because I want them to focus, excel and have fun. But the deal is: If they go to an out-of-state school, they pay part of the differential of what an in-state public college would cost.

JTA – My parents were able to pay for the majority of my education and I helped out. When I graduated and started making money, I paid them back every cent. I did not have to, and they told me not to, but it was something I had to do for myself.

B&GH – In our family we make a deal with our kids: You get the grades to get into any school you care to and we'll pay for it.

*AFM* – When my grandmother died, my family was stunned to learn that she'd secretly squirreled enough money away over the years to pay college tuition and room/board for my brother, sister and me. We earned our spending money. Grandma's gift was a powerful early lesson in the time value of money. We plan to save money for both my children's and my grandchildren's education and pass on her wisdom.

DLS – If you have the means, pay for your kid's college degree. After that it's all up to them.

JMM&RDS – We pay through college, but the kids are on their own for grad school or returning to school later. They should contribute 1/3 of their expenses, we pay 1/3, and the other 1/3 is scholarships, grants or loans if possible.

*AFM* – It's best to get scholarships if you can, but if not then you have to pay. Don't wait until the last minute.

When you have kids, make sure you set up some sort of mechanism that will educate them well either through a trust or some other kind of educational fund. You owe it to your kids to prepare them the best you can for life. Your kids are the most important thing you will leave to the world. Encourage them to save their own money and be candidates for scholarships. At the end of the day, if you have created wealth for yourself and your family, you have an obligation to get your kids educated as well as possible. You can do that by training and developing them to earn it themselves, or by covering some or all of it yourself.

DAS – I split the cost with my parents which gave me an appreciation for the value of an education. We'll use the same strategy with our kid(s).

S&AW – People value what they pay for. Help the kids, especially when they are young, to get great educations.

*AFM* – I always felt bad that my parents paid for my education, but in a few years that money was very little to me in contemporary dollars. For example, after 10 years I was paying as much for cars as my parent's paid for my education. So why would I not just take a loan and pay it off in today's dollars? This is balanced by the fact that my parents felt an obligation to prepare their kids for life and not burden them with debt. Taking loans or having the parent's pay is a hard decision.

RME – I cover all their expenses except for what they do for fun. They must earn that on their own.

DTA – In my case a previous generation wanted to pay for it. 529's will cover it. I will do the same for my grand kids. My kid's must meet my expectations though. They need to know what major they want to be focused on and try to stick to it.

*AFM* – Fortunately my parent's paid for mine. I'm saving every month for my kids.

AC – Teach your kids to be resourceful. This will age me, but when I got accepted to business school, I went to the library and researched potential scholarships that I might apply for. I found one, applied and won a partial scholarship. I also attended undergrad on an ROTC scholarship.

DES – Use real estate as your kid's college fund. Save enough money to put a down payment of a condo or a house. Sell the house when it is worth enough to pay for all the schooling. I know of several parents who have done this for their children.

### *Student loans*

*AFM* – Incurring some educational loan debt is better than not getting an education. Children need financial assistance today given the high cost of education and cost of living.

*AFM* – Try to avoid them. I really wouldn't really want my kids to be massively in debt when they are first out in the real world (or ever!).

*AFM* – One question: Will the job your child gets with the degree they are seeking be able to pay off the loans they are taking out for college and allow them to eat and save money?

*AFM* – Only put books and tuition on student loans. Don't let your kids finance *your* lifestyle with *their* student loans while they are in college. Let them live in low-cost college housing and get by with part-time jobs and a cheap car so they can appreciate what it takes to have their own lifestyle once they get out.

### 529 educational savings plans

*DEFINITION: A 529 Plan is an education savings plan operated by a state or educational institution designed to help families set aside funds for future college costs. As long as the plan satisfies a few basic requirements, the federal tax law provides special tax benefits to the plan participant (Section 529 of the Internal Revenue Code). 529 plans are usually categorized as either prepaid or savings, although some have elements of both. Every state now has at least one 529 plan available. It's up to each state to decide whether it will offer a 529 plan (or possibly more than one), and what it will look like. Educational institutions can offer a 529 prepaid plan but not a 529 savings plan (the private-college Independent 529 Plan is the only institution-sponsored 529 plan thus far). (Source: Bankrate.com)*

R&DW – 529's are a great way to invest and get tax-free growth. You can also gift annually and build up to the current amount needed and let tax-free growth offset the increased cost of education between now and when needed.

S&AW – For college, make your kids play a role in financing their future. The 529 plan shouldn't cover 100%.

SR&BS – Just tuck it away for them early.

MG&DG – Start early by setting up a monthly savings plan.

T&RR – We're doing 529 plans for our kids and all of their cousins and second cousins. Education is the way we've chosen to "spread the wealth" to the extended family.

AA – Set aside your children's college funds as quickly as possible after you make your "nest egg" (before they turn 10). Purchase a 529 Plan, which allows income in the fund to appreciate without taxation. These are very flexible.

BEH – Oddly enough, the 529 accounts I set up for my kids are currently some of our best performers.

*In Lehman's Terms:*
## YOUNG FRUGAL MILLIONAIRES-IN-TRAINING

As long as we are on the topic of education, two frugal millionaires have been helping their sons get a financial education that typically isn't taught in schools.

At an early age, the son of one frugal millionaire wanted to know more about stocks. This frugal millionaire taught his son what to look for when learning about companies and their stocks. The son started doing his own stock research. At age twelve he entered a state wide investment competition...and won it. The son then tried investing with real money (his father's) and netted a $3,000 profit his first time out. The son might be more of a frugal millionaire in the long run than his dad. Good son!

Another frugal millionaire was determined to teach his two sons first hand the value of money and what happens when you save it and it compounds. He put them both to work in his business and paid them a fair wage. Their earnings were put into ROTH IRAs and today those kids can see how money compounds without them having to do a thing. They are already growing their net worth and effortlessly planning for their retirement. The older of the two sons is in college now and deliberately under-spends his monthly allowance so that he can invest and make even more money. Smart kid.

## 23. Trusts / living trusts / wills

Here's a topic that could put most people to sleep, but the frugal millionaires realize that with a little effort they can create various types of protections for themselves and their families. Trusts and wills are not just for the wealthy anymore.

There are countless stories of people that "forgot" to do a will or just didn't get around to it. The families they leave behind have to deal with grief, and a financial mess. There are also stories of families whose personal finances have been exposed to unscrupulous people because their estates weren't set up in a trust and went into probate. All of these situations could have been averted with just a little bit of planning. It costs very little money to set up a revocable family trust and a basic will. You can even do them online if you like.

The frugal millionaires have an interesting array of ideas on how to approach these important legal instruments. They know they are more than just pieces of paper. They are a way to establish a durable legacy.

*REMINDER: 50% of the frugal millionaires had a revocable/living trust in place. It should be 100%! The same should be said for wills. That's more proof that not even the frugal millionaires are perfect.*

### In general

ERK – A very smart way to manage your money. Takes time to figure it out but it's worth the effort.

RJC – An absolute YES. You must protect your assets.

B&GH – Put enough away for your kids to make them safe but not so much that they never have to work for a living. Don't give your kids the money until they're truly adults who've made their own path in life.

JTA – If you don't have and use these, you are an idiot.

JC – Don't put it off. You never know what/when something will happen.

*AFM* – These are a must so that siblings and beneficiaries understand the rules when there is no one to explain them.

JSB – It is important to set up trusts and of course to have wills. All this stuff is very complicated and it's very hard to find attorneys who know what they are doing. Some advice: Write a "Letter of Wishes" to spell out in your own words what you are trying to achieve with your trusts and wills. Discuss how you would prefer likely scenarios to play out after you're gone, but always leave ample wiggle room for your heirs to manage their inheritance as they see fit as you can't foresee everything.

SR&BS – Revisit them every three years – it's amazing how your view of who should get your kids/money/house changes.

MJM – A must have…why not leave what you have worked so hard to acquire to your family or those that YOU choose?

### *Wills*

S&AW – Get a will, if you love your family make their life easier by allowing them to make sense of yours when you are gone.

*AFM* – You must have a will. You can do one online if you are too lazy to hire a lawyer. You never know when your number will come up.

T&RR – No-brainer to have one. Not so easy to determine who and what you want to give and with what strings.

*AFM* – Make sure you have a will and review it regularly. Also have a health care directive and power of attorney set up. Make sure people you name in your will as guardians of your kids agree to do the job upfront.

JT&B – Have them and make sure that your parents do too. They are tough to work through but important.

WCA – Wills are essential.

DTA – Set up a will to protect your kids from themselves.

*AFM* – Write a detailed will. Review it periodically.

### *Trusts*

*AFM* – A revocable trust is important while you are living because you can change it and so that when you are gone you can avoid probate and take care of your relatives.

*DEFINITION: Revocable Trust (which is also referred to as a "revocable living trust") – A trust whereby provisions can be altered or canceled dependent on the grantor. During the life of the trust, income earned is distributed to the grantor, and only after death does property transfer to the beneficiaries.*

*This type of agreement provides flexibility and income to the living grantor; he or she is able to adjust the provisions of the trust and earn income, all the while knowing that the estate will be transferred upon death. These types of trusts avoid having to go through the probate process and therefore protect the family's privacy. (SOURCE: Investopedia.com, with edits)*

BEH – Trusts are a good idea. Most of my assets are in a trust to protect them in the event that someone takes some legal action against me (which becomes more likely if you are perceived to have more money).

*AFM* – Create trusts for your kids, but don't tell them about them, and have them pay out later in life and over time: 1/3 at 35, 1/3 at 40 and 1/3 at 45.

AA – A Charitable Remainder Trust is a wonderful way to create a legacy. Just make sure that you are absolutely willing to part with the money when you place it in the trust.

*DEFINITION: Charitable Remainder Trust – A tax-exempt irrevocable trust designed to reduce the taxable income of individuals by first dispersing income to the beneficiaries of the trust for a specified period of time and then donating the remainder of the trust to the designated charity.*

*The whole idea of a charitable remainder trust is to reduce taxes. This is done by first donating assets into the trust and then having it pay the beneficiary for a stated period of time. Once this time-frame expires, the remainder of the estate is transferred to the charities deemed as beneficiaries. (SOURCE: Investopedia.com)*

*AFM* – A trust is a will that saves you on taxes. It gives you a chance to direct what happens with your money from the grave. It is foolish not to have one. Don't wait. You never know when you will need it. You also don't want to create a bunch of spoiled brats by allowing them to recklessly inherit money. Make sure there are rules and controls in there just as if you were alive and making the decisions.

DTA – Set up a trust to avoid public disclosure of your personal finances.

*AFM* – Use trusts, etc. so that your children will never be a financial burden to their guardians and so the guardians don't bilk your kids out of their own economic security.

### *Lawyers*

DLS – Don't leave what you worked so hard for to the government. Seek a competent trust & estate attorney.

B&GH – Get a professional who knows the state and federal laws really well and tracks the changes all the time.

*AFM* – Get a good lawyer, even if it costs a lot of money. Important!

## 24. Retirement planning

They say that intelligent retirement planning starts before you are born...with your parents. Some people choose not to think about retirement until it's too late. Playing catch-up is tough (although not entirely impossible). The frugal millionaires approach to retirement is balanced with all their other investments, and they have a lot of in-depth ideas on this subject.

### *Philosophies*

VNN – Start early. A small amount of money put away consistently, over time, accumulates into big numbers.

*AFM* – I think investment diversification is critical. Too many people get in trouble because they put everything into one class of investments.

NM&JPR – Don't plan to retire on a pension alone – have a good mix of investments.

*AFM* – To have a great retirement work hard at keeping your marriage healthy and fulfilling. Not only is divorce unhealthy for your emotional and physical well-being, but it also devastates one's finances. Think defensively when it comes to inheritances because of high divorce rates (approximately 50%). You cannot stop your spouse if they want a divorce. Always keep your assets separate; do not co-mingle them with joint marital assets!!! Will your assets to your kids. Otherwise you may see a portion of your estate going to your ex and even to their future spouse and their heirs. That sucks.

*AFM* – Start as early as you can but don't put ALL your money into retirement funds, even if that means not maxing out your 401(k)…Why? You won't be able to touch it until retirement without penalty and you might have many other legitimate financial goals to satisfy earlier.

*DEFINITION: 401(k) – An employer sponsored retirement plan designed to provide tax advantages on an employee's retirement savings. The employer (which is usually a corporation) acts as a fiduciary for the account. The employer is responsible for the establishment of the plan and for the selection of plan investments. Once the plan has been established, the employee defers a portion of his/her annual salary into the fund. (SOURCE: StreetAuthority.com)*

AFM – Use heavier mix of equities when you are younger and more bonds when you are older, a lot older.

DLS – Since you don't know how long you'll live, start living within your means, now.

J&CB – The best thing one can do to prepare for retirement is to remove "stuff" from your life. Instead of "retiring" you free yourself to really enjoy life. In other words when you don't have stuff holding you down there is the opportunity to retire often and whenever you want. Our goal these days is to maintain a small foot print so that we can live large (this is not a money thing). However, most people wait too late in life to realize how much "stuff" is impeding on their happiness.

VTN – People that develop a sense for money, building wealth, investing and retirement planning when they are still in their 20s seem to do well. (Not a scientific view, just my opinion.)

*AFM* – Think about what you will really need in retirement. Don't buy the programs tied to your estimated retirement year if you don't agree with their asset mix. If you want to be aggressive select a retirement year that is farther out than when you really think you will need. Remember that these packaged programs generally have higher fees (you are paying for "convenience" – how does that feel?). You are probably better off with a self selected mix of index and bond funds.

*AFM* – You absolutely need to have other investments going. I like the idea of having a bit of high risk going, not a lot, something you can afford to lose all of and it won't kill you, but if it hits then terrific.

AD – 1) Define and articulate the amount of monies (today's dollars) you will need to live an enjoyable retirement. 2) Don't underestimate taxes. (Think about ordinary income, vs. long/short term capital gains.) 3) Pencil out what your day will look like when you have the extra time on your hands.

*AFM* – Try to formulate exactly "what" retirement means to you. That will help shape how much money you need: staying local, having the kids/grad kids come visit and play golf *likely would take less money than* taking vacations to Europe and skiing every winter in Aspen. It all comes down to tailoring the plan to the goal.

DC – Retirement is a state of mind, and I don't think those who have a full life retire per se' they just stop selling their soul for the almighty dollar. Get a trusted adviser – a good steward of your future – that loves to produce results. That way everyone is skilled and passionate about watching the stock market etc.

### *Strategies*

AA – Set aside a certain dollar amount for retirement with every paycheck and treat is as "untouchable" in a separate bank account.

JDS – The world is flat. Consider retirement in low cost living areas. Thailand anyone?

MW – Plan out what you want to be able to do when you retire and when you want to retire. Then you can see what resources will be necessary. Reduce monthly bills by completely removing revolving credit at an early age, and other loans. Set aside at least 10% of your income when you start working and maintain that through your life so that you can put "your" money to work.

*AFM* – Do not rely on your company stock only. (See: Enron, Bear Stearns, 1990s "dot-bombs.")

DMG – I follow the usual retirement ideas like Roth IRAs.

*DEFINITION: ROTH IRA – Created in 1997 and named for the late Republican Senator William Roth Jr., the Roth IRA functions a little differently than the traditional IRA. Since the Roth IRA is funded with after-tax contributions, there is no allowable tax deduction. However, retired individuals do not have to pay taxes when they take distributions from a Roth IRA. As such, Roth IRAs provide lifelong tax protection. (SOURCE: StreetAuthority.com)*

*AUTHOR'S NOTE: There are income limits and certain restrictions to qualify for setting up and contributing to a Roth IRA. This will depend on your marital status and modified adjusted gross income levels. Check out www.irs.gov for the current regulations. You may also want to look into Roth 401(k) and Roth 403(b) retirement account options. Wikipedia offers a simple explanation of both.*

*AFM* – Always max out your 401(k). Don't buy anything that you don't understand. Minimize your transaction costs (broker's fees, commissions, fund fees, etc.).

WAL – Take a risk and start a business or buy a distressed business and turn it around. If there's good underlying value, but it's poorly managed, there's opportunity to fix it and set yourself up for retirement.

JKB – After 401(k) and IRA contributions, live off 70% of your income and save the rest.

*DEFINITION: Individual Retirement Account (IRA) – A government sponsored personal retirement plan called an. IRAs are tax-advantaged retirement programs for individuals with earned income. In order to open an IRA, an individual must first establish an account with a bank, brokerage firm or mutual fund company. These firms then act in the capacity of a fiduciary. The individual is responsible for establishing the IRA and selecting the plan investments. (SOURCE: StreetAuthority.com, with edits)*

SLL – Two ideas: 1) Even if you can't qualify for Roth IRAs or deductible regular IRAs, you should do the non-deductible IRAs for their tax deferment advantages. Plus under current law, in a few years you will be able to convert both these deductible & non-deductible IRA accounts to Roth IRAs regardless of your income. Hopefully this law won't be repealed or delayed before it takes effect. And, 2) If you are close to taking distributions from your retirement plans, you may want to move a small portion of your underlying investment in these plans into cash (money market funds) in anticipation of these distributions if you think that the market for whatever they are invested in may be higher when you convert to cash than when you need to take the distributions. Be careful here, timing the market in very difficult. Be prudent and don't overdo it.

*AFM* – Make sure you front-load most future charitable donations into a donor-advised fund prior to retirement so that donations will be deductible at maximum marginal rates (while you still have sufficient W-2 income).

WCA – Save as much as possible after fully funding qualified plan opportunities. Have adequate disability insurance. Enjoy life, but don't be the typical American consumer who is so focused on impressing the Joneses.

*AFM* – We are paying off our house as soon as possible, so we can then put more money into retirement.

JC – Hedge against the likely continued erosion of the dollar. Try international mutual funds.

*AFM* – Keep a change jar!  You would be surprised how much it adds up every year and can pay for an extra mortgage payment or vacation which can get you to your retirement goals sooner.

JT&B – We are heavy on the 401(k). Mostly we max out in terms of putting the biggest % towards that. It is fairly diversified – a few general steady funds make up the bulks. We do stocks on our own – not in a 401(k) – and keep cash on our own too – not in a 401(k).

*AFM* – If you are changing states upon retirement, sell all gains prior to leaving a low-state tax state and sell all loses prior to leaving a high-state tax state.

### Real estate strategies

VTN – If you have any way possible to buy some land or a small house in a place you like while still in your 20s, do it. You'll always have it, and even it's really rustic, when you get older, you'll have land you can sell or develop it.

*AFM* – Moving periodically will restart another $500K capital gain exclusion on your primary residence. That will help you boost your retirement nest egg.

*DEFINITION: Capital Gains Exclusion – When you sell your primary residence, you can make up to $250,000 in profit if you're a single owner, or $500,000 if you're married, and not owe any capital gains taxes. You must own and live in the home for two out of the five years before the sale. (SOURCE: Bankrate.com, with edits)*

WAL – Find rental property that is poorly managed and maintained and buy it. It can provide an opportunity for increasing rents and adding appraisal value to the property. You can leverage your money in real estate, whereas stocks or bonds YOU are putting up 100% of the investment.

*AFM* – In the real estate market, having someone make the payments for you, ala rent on a home that you own is also a great long term investment, just be careful where you buy it and what you pay for it.

JMM&DRS – Instead of buying that second or third home and diverting money from the retirement fund (or calling it the retirement fund) consider this: just pay cash for the vacations and sock the extra money away in the retirement fund. Chances are your investments will appreciate more than a rental property and you won't have any maintenance costs.

*AFM* – Invest while you have income in properties or vacation homes now for what you will want/need in retirement. Buy into a home, etc. and rent it till you need it. It's a great investment and you will have it paid for by the time you need it.

*AFM* – Here is an interesting way that I funded *my parent's* retirement using real estate: My parents sold us their house in this very complicated, tax minimizing way. First, start with 3 siblings, I am one of them. My husband and I could afford to buy my parents $1 million home and we paid them $666,000. Then my parents and I paid my other two siblings and their family members $333,000 (total to each family) in $10K "gift" increments ($10K was the maximum at the time this was done). The end result is $0 inheritance tax on the house when my parents die. Make sense? My brothers (the two other siblings) got money for their kid's college when they needed it, my parents got some cash for their house and would continue to live there, and we take over the house after they die.

RME – As mentioned earlier, I have 4 pieces of real estate; two condos near universities, where my children live at this time, an office building where I work, and my home. My plan is to downsize our 4 bedroom – 3 bath home to a 2 bedroom – 2 bath home once both children are married. As long as the condos remain rentable I'll keep them maintained and if/when the market goes out of control again then I will sell them.

B&GH – Given today's economy, don't count on your primary residence increasing in value as part of your retirement nest egg.

JC – Try purchasing real estate overseas to continue to hedge against the likely continued erosion of the dollar.

### *Hiring financial experts*

JSB – Unless you really know what you're doing with your retirement plan, and have the time to devote to it (at least daily) don't run your own retirement portfolio. Let a pro do it. You can talk to the pro and give them tips/instructions in areas you are expert in (like your industry segment) but let them manage the day-to-day, and the selling and rebalancing. And by "pro," I don't mean "broker." Brokers are hopelessly conflicted and their incentives are all wrong – (the major incentive is to trade, not to make money). The frugal millionaire needs a money manager with zero conflicts and a long term strategic view. Increasingly, this does not include the firms who have now developed so many internal products that they have become rife with conflicts – and the performance of their wealth management programs over the past 5 years shows it. This thinking probably also applies to real estate investments.

*AFM* – Retirement Planning Tips:

1) Create a plan working with, but not blindly relying on, a reputable fee-based third party you trust. They should provide objectivity and question your sanity when needed.
2) Review the plan at least annually.
3) Know what you own and why you own it.
4) Have a disciplined plan to sell and stick to it (see 1 above) and take the emotion out of your investment decisions.
5) Make sure you have a will and review/revise it regularly.

6) Term life insurance is all most people ever need.

7) Repeat after me: a broker is a salesman, a broker is a salesman...

FJC – Have your retirement plan created and managed by a professional financial planner.

*AFM* – Have an expert prepare a model which forecasts your cash balance through your likely lifetime so you can set limits on your spending. You determine what you want to have left when you die (could be zero, could be something to leave for kids), you estimate your lifespan, and you can calculate what you can spend each year starting with your current net worth. Also, you never know when you'll have a heart attack or stroke. So if you are thinking retirement, make sure you have an estate plan in the event that you don't live through your retirement.

*AFM* – Seek the advice of a fee based, not commission based, advisor. Get recommendations from at least two advisors and seriously consider the ones in common.

JTA – First, plan to live to 100 years old. Figure out what it will really cost you to live that long (monthly and annually) with inflation and the cost of prescription drugs which we will all need as we live longer. I also believe it is good to lock in a rate in your early 50's for long term extended health care as many people will live longer due to advances in medicine but our mind will go first. It will be terrible to drain our own bank accounts as well as our children trying to pay for Alzheimer care.

## *In Lehman's Terms:*
## SMART RETIREMENT PLANNING

One frugal millionaire decided to take his money and have fun "spending" it in a way that many non-millionaires would not generally think about. This particular frugal millionaire loves boating and the water, so he spent months having fun researching opportunities to buy a little beach getaway.

He ended up making a smart buy of a home right on the water, with a boat lift. He'll tell you it's nothing fancy, but it suits his lifestyle perfectly. This project allowed him to enjoy spending his money, but on something that would create rental income and appreciate in value over the years before he retires to it.

It also fit his life-style goals of wanting to spend more time wearing sandals and Hawaiian shirts.

---

# CHAPTER VI

# Creating the *model* frugal millionaire

─────────────

Now you know that it's true. The frugal millionaires do think differently about money than the rest of us. At least the 70 that participated in this study do…and there are many more out there just like them. They have learned to embrace things about growing wealth that most of the population isn't interested in or hasn't thought about yet. If you don't think about it you can't make it happen.

At the beginning of the book I mentioned that not one frugal millionaire had every great idea in each of the 24 categories that were covered. They all, however, have been highly successful in their own unique ways using a wide range of ideas.

After reviewing over 800 of their ideas, a number of powerful best practices emerged. They were used to create the *model* frugal millionaire. These are the fundamentals necessary for growing wealth and they are as close to perfection as we can get. When used all together they can be very powerful.

The great news is that anyone (including other millionaires) should be able to apply these best practices to their own personal financial situations and grow their wealth. Just take the initiative to get started, and go for it. Try a few and see how they work for you.

Here then are the top fifteen wealth growing best practices that someone striving to be a *model* frugal millionaire would love to embrace:

1. **They would love the stock market**...
   because they grow with the market by investing primarily in Index Funds that have extremely low management fees. These funds track to the major market indices like the S&P 500, Wilshire 5000, Russell 2000, and EAFE international stocks etc., and they are easy to follow. The *model* frugal millionaire works with their financial advisors to keep their investing patient, simple and inexpensive because it really doesn't need to be that complicated. They balance their investments with retirement vehicles like a 401k, an IRA and/or a Roth IRA, and accept more risky investments based on their risk tolerance.

2. **They would love real estate and mortgages**...
   because they use them to create even more wealth. They only use 15 or 30 year fixed mortgages that are very predictable and then they accelerate the pay-off as soon as they can. They know that this "good debt" can help them. They get the smallest mortgage they possibly can and live below their means in a reasonably sized house. They realize that their house is more of a place to live than an investment while they are in it, and if they own any other real estate it has to be income producing.

3. **They would love new cars and car leases...**
   because they pick out the type of new car they
   want years in advance and buy it used after it
   comes off a lease that someone else signed up for.
   They can get an affordable deal on a great, efficient car that still has some warranty on it, and
   they let someone else eat all the big depreciation.
   They pay cash and keep it for a long time.

4. **They would love credit cards...**
   because they know how to leverage them perfectly. They have as few of them as possible (one with
   a big credit limit is usually good enough) and
   don't overspend on them. They pay them off every
   month. They never pay an interest charge but
   they get all the perks. They don't like the "credit"
   part, but they do love the "card" part. They treat
   the card like they are using cash, and they don't
   part with *that* without a really good reason.

5. **They would love spending big money...**
   but they don't spend it on "stuff." Instead they
   spend money on investments that make even
   more money for them: like appreciating assets or
   retirement plans. Simply put, they opt for investment spending instead of consumer spending. It's
   still the thrill of spending after all...just chan-
   neled in a more profitable direction. While they
   still have fun with their money, they tend to give
   themselves rewards after they have made their
   fortunes, not before.

6. **They would love conserving and recycling...**
   not only because it's green and good for the planet, but because it keeps them from wasting

things, and that helps them make money. Not wasting anything is always a smart strategy. They know that being able to afford to waste is not an excuse to waste. When they learn not to waste one thing (like money) they tend to not waste anything else.

7. **They would love giving to others**...
   and donating to efficient causes and charities that matter to them. They *all* do this. Usually it is money, but sometimes it is time or things. Either way they know they have an obligation to give back and they do so... generously. When they give back, they know they also get back...even more. They often give donations as holiday gifts in the name of family and friends instead of stuff that will be re-gifted, forgotten or never used.

8. **They would love health and exercise**...
   because without it they have nothing, no matter how wealthy they are. They opt for healthy lifestyles (such as not smoking), and smart medical care and they don't make their pursuit of any of this all that complicated. For exercise they simply go out their front door and take a walk, run or a bicycle ride.

9. **They would love lawyers and accountants**...
   because these professionals can efficiently create wills, trusts, revocable trusts, LLCs, corporations and other instruments that help them protect and grow their assets, and then pass them on. They know that spending here is a preventive investment.

10. **They would love marriage, and the pre-nups that go with them**...

so that they can focus on love first, then money. They typically only marry people who share the same relationship with money that they do. They stay married. They have a life plan and begin executing it well ahead of their retirement.

11. **They would love great clothes**...

because they buy high quality traditional classics that look good and last for years. They wait to buy them on sale and they don't make a sport out of shopping.

12. **They would love traveling**...

but they do it efficiently, by using miles from the credit cards that they never pay interest charges on. They are willing to travel slightly off season. They also search for great travel deals online or offline, wherever these deals may be.

13. **They would love eating great food**...

but they do it mostly at home, with friends and family. They will eat "out" to celebrate great accomplishments and milestones but they do it in moderately priced restaurants, and they tip generously. They might even bring their favorite wine along as well.

14. **They would love trendy gadgets**...

not because they buy them personally, but because they look at the company that is behind them to see if there is an investment opportunity. (Think: Apple iPods, Samsung HDTVs, Sony Handycams, and Nintendo Wii's, etc.) They can buy plenty of gadgets later (and if they do, they wait until the kinks are worked out and they are less expensive) with the money they make off of the stocks that they buy in these companies.

15. **They would love "nickel and dime you to death" daily spending**...
that is, as long as someone else is doing it, like buying: fancy coffee drinks, cigarettes, afternoon snacks, bottled water, shopping for stuff they won't ever use, constantly eating meals out, buying fuel for gas-wasting vehicles, etc. Chances are they have invested in the companies that are providing those goods and services that 98% of the population can't seem to get enough of.

And ultimately, they would love the piece of mind and freedom that doing all the above gives them...because it helps them to feel safe and happy, and continue to grow their wealth. That is their dream, and they live it every day.

*In Lehman's Terms:*
## IN SEARCH OF
## THE AMERICAN DREAM

What exactly is the American Dream? It must be something special because it returns over 7,000,000 hits on Google.

For many people it's that they have a good job, a safe place to live, their kids get a good education, and they are able to retire comfortably.

For others, that dream has instead become disfigured into: "I must over extend myself financially to show everyone around me that I am successful and better off than they are...I must not just keep up with the Jones, I must annihilate and humiliate them!" As you might guess, this usually creates the potential for financial ruin. I don't personally know the Joneses, and I don't ever want to. Do you? Chances are pretty good that they are broke anyway!

There are many versions of "The American Dream;" for the frugal millionaires in this book it is financial freedom, safety, security, and being able to do what they want to do with their personal lives. It took a lot of patience and effort for these people to get to where they are today. For them, it's not about living beyond their means and trying to impress others with how many depreciating assets they can buy with consumer debt. The frugal millionaires have created a different American Dream than many of us.

Have you thought about your American Dream lately?

---

# CHAPTER VII

# Money mottoes

Everyone, it seems, has a motto they live by. Naturally, many of the frugal millionaires have money mottoes that they live by (among other life mottoes). If you need a little inspiration maybe there's one here that fits your style. Feel free to borrow them, adapt them and make them your own.

*AFM* – I have nothing to prove to anyone but myself.

FJC – It's not how much you make, it's what you do with it.

RDF – No matter how much money you have, someone will always have more. Deal with it and enjoy your life.

RJC – Before you buy something, wait and see if in a month you still want it. If it appreciates, think about it. If it depreciates, walk away.

JSB – Don't be afraid to enjoy your money!

R&DW – Enjoy your life and family today vs. only thinking toward the time you believe you will have enough money to start enjoying it. While financial security is important, and you worked hard for it, it can't give back lost time.

J&CB – Money, like education, gives us choices, and choices are more valuable than anything.

*AFM* – Money doesn't really buy true happiness as the mind tends to gravitate towards other needs once wealth is achieved. It really isn't the best measure of success anyway.

JDS – You can't save your way to prosperity.

DES – Take an educated risk and make it pay off.

*AFM* – Really understand what you want out of life and *work* your money towards that.

*AFM* – Save, Save, Save…Unless you see that "must have item" and if you can truly afford it, then buy it!

*AFM* – Make a budget – Stick to it!

*AFM* – Money is a tool that needs to be used with respect and caution.

*AFM* – Money, like religion, can bring out the best and worst in people.

JLL – Do what you love and the money will take care of itself.

B&GH – Your money should work for you, you shouldn't work for your money.

*AFM* – Spend and save knowing that any day your health and quality of life could change dramatically.

*AFM* – Spend on life experiences that are with you until the day you die.

*AFM* – Don't get "nickeled and dimed" to death financially.

JTA – Debt will kill you.

DC – A dollar saved is two dollars earned.

*AFM* – Live simply. Invest early and over a long period of time.

RP – You can't always get what you want. But if you try sometime you might just find, you get what you need. *(Borrowed with respect, from Mick Jagger.)*

AA – You are rich if you spend less than you take in...

DLS – No matter how much money you have, live below your means.

*AFM* – Money is freedom, and whether freedom is good depends on what you make of it.

*AFM* – Be careful with your money, but have fun too.

DES – People want money because they think it buys freedom, but you rarely need as much as you think.

S&AW – Be willing to treat yourself, or it *(the money)* isn't worth accumulating.

DTA – Financial defense wins out over financial offense.

AC – Figure out what you really want and spend money to do it right. A gold-plated wheelchair won't matter.

VRN – It's how you share money with others that makes it the most valuable commodity in the end, sharing it brings more back to you.

VTN – Your money should work harder than you do.

*AFM* – Figure out your "money number," execute on your plan to hit it, and enjoy your life along the way.

JT&B – A penny saved is a penny earned…if you can keep it in your pocket!

———————————

## CHAPTER VIII

# Prized possessions

The frugal millionaires now get to show you part of their fun side: their prized possessions. If the below were a list of all the toys that ONE millionaire had the media would be all over them. Sorry, but this list of prized possessions is spread over the entire frugal millionaires group.

Each frugal millionaire was asked what their prized possession was. Not all chose to answer. For all the money these people have they put a premium on possessions that have special meaning to them. They don't buy stuff just to have stuff.

*REMINDER: The frugal millionaires have been million-aires for an average of 9 years.*

Now, consider this: They have owned their prized posses-sions for an average of 7 years. That means that, on aver-age, they waited until they were millionaires to make these acquisitions. Delayed gratification is one key to financial success. They didn't take significant amounts of money out of their income streams or investment funds while they were accumulating wealth to buy these prized possessions. If they did there is a good chance they wouldn't be million-aires today.

The question posed to the frugal millionaires was: "What is your most prized "personal luxury item" that you have bought, regardless of what it cost (or how much it costs to maintain)?"

Their answers were (in no particular order):

Piano, Leica camera collection, full carbon road bicycle, 1959 Porsche convertible, 50' sailboat, Coach bag, overcoat made by a Vermont artisan, wine collection, 42' Sea Ray powerboat, Myth TV DVR, BMW 3 Series convertible, 6 Series BMW, 1993 Saab convertible, primary home, man's fur coat, second home, 46" Samsung LCD HDTV, oil painting, sailboat, African tribal mask collection, former astronaut's OMEGA space watch, computer, 57" HDTV, 1989 Porsche triple-black 911 slantnose cabriolet, vacation home, art, antiques, powerboat, Mercedes, ski condo, airplane, home, 2007 Corvette convertible, 2007 Jeep Wrangler Rubicon, 2007 Corvette Z06, Ferrari F430, 1950's OMEGA man's watch, home stereo, and a swimming pool.

A 1993 Saab convertible?

They have some neat things, but their lives don't revolve around them. They did give insights into what motivated them to buy these items.

- 89% said their purchase was emotionally driven.
- 69% said they negotiated a good price.
- 56% said they would consider selling it.
- 51% said they bought it because they wanted it, regardless of the price (within reason).
- 14% said they had no "prized possession" at all.

- 7% said that pets, travel, relationships and personal hand-made gifts from parents were their prized possessions. They would not give these up.

The fact that the frugal millionaires have these prized possessions isn't what made them millionaires. It's what's in their bank accounts, investment portfolios, and real estate holdings that made them millionaires. This is where so many people get it wrong. They think that owning these possessions is the secret key that opens the door to millionaire-ville. It doesn't.

---

## CHAPTER IX

# Final thoughts

Seventy frugal millionaires just gave you their ideas about money in a straightforward and uncut way. Some of their ideas may seem very simple to you. You might have even thought of many of them on your own. Now try doing them. That's what will make the difference.

These frugal millionaires are everyday people, but with one significant difference, they happen to think differently about money than most other people do, and because of that they've grown their wealth dramatically. That's all. That's it. It's all very simple.

If success in buying real estate is all about *location, location, location* then success in growing wealth is all about *execution, execution, execution*.

The frugal millionaires are in the minority and you can join them. They would love to have more frugal millionaire friends to hang out with. What has worked for them could work for you...the difference between them and so many other people is that they have made these ideas happen and they have stuck with them.

We are all very similar in our financial goals when it comes right down to it. Try some of the ideas the frugal millionaires have given you – or – try some of the best practices of the *model* frugal millionaire. If you think they will work for you, then talk to a trusted advisor or mentor and use them, just like the frugal millionaires do everyday.

If you are thinking, "these people are already millionaires of course they can do this stuff effortlessly," well, think again. As you know, almost all of them started out with middle class upbringings. Some were even poor. They didn't become frugal after they became millionaires...they started the process of being frugal long before now and it helped them get to where they are today. You can too. You just have to want to do it. I know you can do it. After a while it becomes a part of the way you think. And that's when the real fun begins. .

You now have more ideas and best practices to use to grow wealth for yourself than you did before you read this book.

Be smart with your money. Don't waste it. And, be frugal – 'til you're satisfied!

———————

# About the author

Jeff Lehman is a former media executive, an entrepreneur, and author. *The Frugal Millionaires* is his second book.

Jeff's father took him to his first shareholder meeting at the age of thirteen. (That's a great way to start your teen years according to his dad.) From that point on he was interested in the idea of investing and being smart with money.

He has made slightly more "smart" decisions about money than "dumb" ones and is grateful to have so many brilliant and wealthy people around him to constantly learn from.

Jeff grew up in Coral Gables, Florida and earned his BSBA and MBA from the University of Central Florida in Orlando.

He "gives back" by helping mentor business students at the University of Central Florida and the University of Washington.

Jeff is an avid sailor who has competed in a transatlantic yacht race. He has also studied architecture and law. He lives in Seattle, Washington.

Contact him at: author@TheFrugalMillionaires.com.